MANAGING
WORRY
AND
ANXIETY

MANAGING
WORRY
AND
ANXIETY

PRACTICAL TOOLS TO HELP YOU
DEAL WITH LIFE'S CHALLENGES

JEAN HOLTHAUS,
LISW, LMSW

Revell

a division of Baker Publishing Group
Grand Rapids, Michigan

© 2020 by Jean Holthaus

Published by Revell
a division of Baker Publishing Group
PO Box 6287, Grand Rapids, MI 49516-6287
www.revellbooks.com

Printed in the United States of America

Library of Congress Cataloging-in-Publication Data
Names: Holthaus, Jean, 1963– author.
Title: Managing worry and anxiety : practical tools to help you deal with life's challenges / Jean Holthaus, LISW, LMSW.
Description: Grand Rapids : Revell, a division of Baker Publishing Group, 2020.
Identifiers: LCCN 2019027592 | ISBN 9780800736071 (paperback)
Subjects: LCSH: Worry—Religious aspects—Christianity. | Anxiety—Religious aspects—Christianity.
Classification: LCC BV4908.5 .H65 2020 | DDC 152.4/6—dc23
LC record available at https://lccn.loc.gov/2019027592

Unless otherwise indicated, Scripture quotations are from the Holy Bible, New International Version®. NIV®. Copyright © 1973, 1978, 1984, 2011 by Biblica, Inc.™ Used by permission of Zondervan. All rights reserved worldwide. www.zondervan .com. The "NIV" and "New International Version" are trademarks registered in the United States Patent and Trademark Office by Biblica, Inc.™

Scripture quotations labeled NASB are from the New American Standard Bible® (NASB), copyright © 1960, 1962, 1963, 1968, 1971, 1972, 1973, 1975, 1977, 1995 by The Lockman Foundation. Used by permission. www.Lockman.org

The content of this book was prepared and written by Jean Holthaus, LISW, LMSW, in her personal capacity. The opinions expressed in this publication are the author's own and do not necessarily reflect the views of Pine Rest Christian Mental Health Services.

This publication is intended to provide helpful and informative material on the subjects addressed. Readers should consult their personal health professionals before adopting any of the suggestions in this book or drawing inferences from it. The author and publisher expressly disclaim responsibility for any adverse effects arising from the use or application of the information contained in this book.

20   21   22   23   24   25   26   7   6   5   4   3   2   1

For all those who long to experience God's
"peace that passes understanding."

(Phil. 4:7)

CONTENTS

ACKNOWLEDGMENTS

While this book contains one author's name, it is actually a compilation created by many authors who have composed lines and woven them into the fabric of my soul. The tapestry of my life has been formed, redeemed, and made beautiful beyond anything I could have imagined by their presence, their love, and their words of truth and affirmation. Some have woven strong threads through large sections of the tapestry while others added thin, sparkling threads, giving richness and depth. I can't identify and name each author, but all are important and I am grateful for the sacrifice, love, and investment each has made.

First and foremost, I am grateful for Jesus who relentlessly and passionately pursued me from the moment I drew my first breath. He was unwilling to leave me bereft of love and serving the tyrannical god I believed him to be. His persistent love has changed my life. I can't imagine life without my kinsman redeemer, bridegroom, and friend.

My children, Michelle and Michael, have taught me what it means to love and be loved in ways I never dreamed possible. Michelle, you have been a creative artist since you were old enough to give voice to the music in your head from your car seat. You are an amazing, loving woman who has taught me invaluable lessons about what it is to be an artist. Michael, your tenacity has both brought you through dark times and allowed you to embrace adventure and live life fully. You have boldly struck out into uncharted waters repeatedly in the course of your life. I am both awestruck and challenged by your example. Thank you both for extending grace and forgiveness as I have learned and continue to learn what it means to mother.

Both Suzanne Vogel and Michael Hirsch have been sojourners with me on the journey to find healing and wholeness. I am thankful for their commitment to journey together and grateful for their spouses as well. Sojourning with me required sacrifices from each of them at times that weren't always convenient. Michael, there isn't much of life we haven't done together in some fashion. I am thankful we are both similar enough to "get" one another and different enough to challenge and balance one another. Thank you for the countless hours spent sharing life, sacrificially giving of yourself, and just having fun together. I am so glad you are my brother and we learned to be friends instead of competitors! Suzanne, *friend* is simply too small of a word to describe your role in my life. I am eternally grateful God brought you into my life and you were willing to extend love. You have challenged me, boldly spoken truth, and passionately encouraged me to become who God created me to be rather than settling for being what I could see. Your wisdom, passion, creativity, and steadfast faithfulness are woven throughout the tapestry of my life and the lives of everyone who knows you. I cherish the honest, vulnerable, covenantal relationship we forged on the journey as it has forever changed me.

Paul Hietbrink, you taught me what a father's heart looks like and what it feels like to be fathered. You embodied the wisdom and love of the Father in ways that gave me tangible experiences of things I could previously not even conceive of. Thank you for seeing beauty in the ashes.

Lee Luhrs, Cal Meuzelaar, and Rita Schacherer, you have each been mentors and teachers along the way who have taken risks and invested in me personally and professionally. You each model what it means to be a therapist and have allowed me to know you well enough to emulate what I observe.

Andrea Doering, this book started with an email from you asking if I had ever thought about writing. It felt surreal then and still feels that way today. I am indebted to you for seeing potential, guiding me through this process, encouraging me, and helping to make my writing better.

Meghan Hirsch, you spent hours turning my cryptic annotations into appropriate documentation, correcting formatting errors, and pointing out sentences that made no sense. Your time has been invaluable, and I appreciate your attention to detail!

Finally, one does not leave graduate school knowing how to be a therapist. The thousands of people who have sat across from me in my office over the last twenty-four years have been the teachers through whom I have learned to be present and to connect with people in the midst of their anguish and their joy. The time I spent walking with and learning from people as they found ways to effectively manage mental health issues fashioned and formed me into a therapist. Thank you for allowing me to share in your journey and learn from each of you. Without you, this book would not be possible.

CHAPTER ONE

WORRY OR ANXIETY?

Is another book about anxiety really necessary? I found my-self weighing this question as I contemplated writing this book. While I pondered, three different articles were pub-lished nationwide indicating anxiety was on the rise within both children and adults. During the same brief time period, I was also contacted by a local school superintendent struggling to know how to help the elementary students within the district manage anxiety effectively. This superintendent was highly concerned that even kindergarten students were struggling with increased symptoms of anxiety and wanted to provide students with skills to effectively lower anxiety. All this, in addition to the fact that about half of my therapy caseload is comprised of clients strug-gling with anxiety, highlighted the fact anxiety is an increasing problem in our society, creating difficulty for both individuals and organizations.

My goal in writing this book is to help you, the reader, under-stand what anxiety is, what causes anxiety, and what resources you can call upon to help manage anxiety. As a therapist, I have found simplistic explanations of anxiety and how it should be "cured" to be highly ineffective. In fact, many of the people who find their way to my office have been demoralized by their inability to effectively engage their willpower and just "stop it." Thus, this book will not contain simple explanations or solutions.

Anxiety exhibits itself in multiple ways, there are many factors that contribute to its presence, and it has no known "cure." However, there are resources and skills that can be utilized to effectively manage anxiety so it does not interfere with your ability to live a fulfilling and productive life.

Part of the difficulty associated with anxiety stems from how the word has been and continues to be used. The term *anxiety* is a catchall description for symptoms ranging from normal thoughts, feelings, and physical sensations experienced in an unfamiliar situation to symptoms associated with a severe and debilitating mental illness. Imagine how confusing it would be if saying "I'm diabetic" could either mean you are experiencing a sugar rush after indulging in a decadent piece of cheesecake or you need insulin immediately to avoid lapsing into a life-threatening coma.

Anxiety is a term much like the term *blood sugar*—it describes certain thoughts, feelings, and physical sensations just as blood sugar describes certain chemicals within the body. Everyone has blood sugar, and it is considered normal if it stays within a certain range. When it leaves the "normal" range, that is a medical condition requiring treatment for the individual involved to return to health. Similarly, everyone experiences anxiety, and it is healthy if it stays within a certain range. When anxiety exceeds the "normal" range it becomes a debilitating medical condition requiring treatment, just like any other medical condition, for the individual experiencing it to return to health.

Healthy Anxiety

The human body is created to physically respond when placed in intense situations. As you walk into a job interview, your heart rate and breathing pick up a bit, increasing the flow of oxygen to your brain and allowing you to think more quickly and clearly. This physical response helps you to adapt to an intense situation and perform optimally. Healthy anxiety equips you to function better in difficult situations.

Healthy anxiety triggers what is commonly referred to as "fight-flight-freeze," a set of automatic responses designed to help you effectively cope with situations perceived as dangerous. For example:

> **Fight:** your teenage son is driving 55 mph going into a curve marked 45 mph, and you yell at him from the passenger side of the car (fight) to get him to slow down.
>
> **Flight:** two of your coworkers begin shouting at one another and you find yourself exiting the room as quickly as possible (flight).
>
> **Freeze:** you see a snake in the corner and stand perfectly still staring at it as it slithers away (freeze).

When you encounter something potentially dangerous, your brain rapidly changes in several ways; the prefrontal cortex is bypassed and your body draws upon the limbic system as it responds. The prefrontal cortex is the part of your brain that:

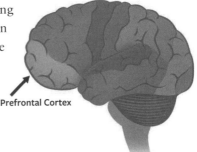

Prefrontal Cortex

- makes decisions
- plans complex behaviors

- sorts out conflicting thoughts
- determines what is good and bad
- makes sure your choices move you toward your goals
- determines whether a thought is socially appropriate to act upon
- determines the long-term consequences of a behavior

The limbic system, on the other hand, is located in the middle of our head and is composed of several parts that are always on alert for anything that might harm us. This limbic system functions much like a home security system—when it senses danger it sounds the alarm, and our body immediately kicks into high alert. When the alarm goes off, our

- heart races
- breathing becomes shallow
- muscles become tense and ready for action
- startle response becomes intensely sensitive to any movement or noise

Limbic System

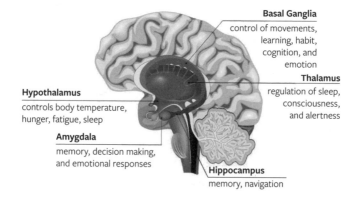

Basal Ganglia
control of movements, learning, habit, cognition, and emotion

Thalamus
regulation of sleep, consciousness, and alertness

Hypothalamus
controls body temperature, hunger, fatigue, sleep

Amygdala
memory, decision making, and emotional responses

Hippocampus
memory, navigation

These changes happen without any conscious thought on our part and physically prepare our body to fight off the attack, run away from the threat, or freeze and hope it will go away.

The fight, flight, or freeze response to potential threats is necessary and allows us to react quickly and appropriately when danger approaches. This is healthy anxiety—your brain correctly identifies something that could produce harm and your body prepares to deal with this potential threat. Once the threat has been appropriately dealt with, the anxiety dissipates, and you return to your former level of functioning.

The Worry Zone

Healthy anxiety varies in intensity, duration, and expression, but is a response to potential danger. Once this danger has been addressed, the anxiety dissipates. However, many of us move past healthy anxiety into what I would call the "worry zone."

Worry can be defined as persistently thinking about problems, fears, or concerns because you think something bad has happened or could happen. Worry differs from healthy anxiety in that it is driven by an internal thought process instead of a reaction to external stimuli. If I am driving a car in a snowstorm, the anxiety my body feels is related to the physical circumstances, and, when I arrive safely at home, my anxiety will dissipate because my circumstances have changed. However, if I am sitting at work, it begins to snow, and I begin to think of all the things that might happen as I try to drive home, I have moved from healthy anxiety into worry. Many clients announce to me that they "are worriers"

or were "born a worrier," and I always respond by asking the same question: "Have you ever seen an infant worry?" Inevitably this brings about a laugh as the client acknowledges babies don't worry. Worry is learned and is born out of the belief that if you think enough about all the things that "might" happen, you will be better prepared if they do happen or will be able to prevent them from happening altogether.

Worry creates a constant feeling of uneasiness and results in being overly concerned about a situation or potential problem. Worry forces your mind and your body to remain in overdrive, making you intensely sensitive and concerned that anything and anyone might be a potential threat. Worry makes it difficult to focus on reality or to think clearly.

The primary difference between worry and healthy anxiety is its focus. Worry is focused on the different things that *might* happen. A worrier plays out all the different things that *could* possibly happen tomorrow and attempts to figure out how to handle each of these scenarios while lying in bed the night before. Both worry and healthy anxiety trigger the same chemical reactions physiologically. In both cases, the body gears up to

Body Reactions in Fight/Flight/Freeze

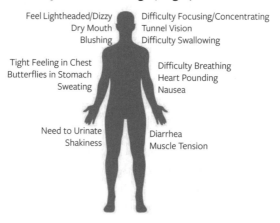

Feel Lightheaded/Dizzy
Dry Mouth
Blushing

Difficulty Focusing/Concentrating
Tunnel Vision
Difficulty Swallowing

Tight Feeling in Chest
Butterflies in Stomach
Sweating

Difficulty Breathing
Heart Pounding
Nausea

Need to Urinate
Shakiness

Diarrhea
Muscle Tension

fight, flee, or freeze—incredibly helpful responses if there is a car coming at you in traffic but not helpful if you are attempting to sleep at night. Worry's focus on the future and what might happen makes it difficult for the body to know when the threat has passed so the body remains "on alert" and controlled by the limbic system instead of the prefrontal cortex (where decision making occurs).

Worry, like healthy anxiety, causes the limbic system to release stress hormones like cortisol into the body. As these hormones enter the blood stream, they produce the responses you see in the diagram above. Unlike healthy anxiety, worry often persists for extended periods of time. Elevated stress hormones within the body over long periods of time negatively impact the body in significant ways. The American Medical Association has stated that stress is the basic cause of more than 60 percent of all human illnesses and diseases.[1] The diagram below shows how stress adversely affects virtually every system in the body over time.

The stress produced by worry can be devastating emotionally, spiritually, and physically. Worry is what Paul was referring to in Scripture when he said, "Do not be anxious about anything" (Phil. 4:6). Unlike healthy anxiety, which is necessary, or medical

Impact of Stress

Skin:
Increased Acne and Other Skin Issues

Brain:
Depression, Anxiety, Irritability, Impaired Memory, Headaches

Heart:
High Blood Pressure and Cholesterol, Increased Heart Rate, Heart Attacks

Joints/Muscles:
Lower Bone Density, Increased Pain, Muscle Tension

Intestinal:
Stomach Cramps, Reflux, Nausea, Weight Gain/Loss, Diarrhea, Irritable Bowel Syndrome, Constipation

Immune:
Compromised Immune System, Increased Illness, Increased Recovery Time

Reproduction:
Decreased Sex Drive, Lower Sperm Count, Increased Menstrual Pain

Pancreas:
Diabetes

illnesses we do not cause, worry is a habit within our control and Scripture tells us to avoid it.

While you may feel like you were "born a worrier," it is a learned pattern of behavior and, like all behaviors, can be changed. Changing it involves hard work and time. Many of the strategies talked about in the second half of this book can be utilized to conquer worry.

Anxiety Disorders

Every human being is born with healthy anxiety—babies react to unexpected loud noises just as adults do. Many of us learn to worry as we grow and gradually make this an integral part of daily life. Eighteen percent of the population find themselves experiencing more than normal anxiety or even worry. Every year, forty million adults in the United States suffer from an anxiety-related mental illness.[2] Anxiety disorders are highly treatable yet only 36.9 percent of those with an anxiety disorder receive treatment.[3] To give some perspective to these statistics, forty million adults have a diagnosable anxiety disorder and only thirty million adults have diagnosable diabetes.[4] While 36.9 percent of those with anxiety don't receive treatment, only 23.8 percent of those with diabetes don't receive treatment.[5] So, more people are ill with anxiety and fewer of them receive treatment. How can this be?

Until the development of Magnetic Resonance Imaging (MRI) in the 1970s and the Functional MRI in 1990, scientists and doctors didn't have technology that allowed them to determine how the brain functioned. Prior to this, most of what was known about the brain was conjecture mixed with what could be learned through autopsies. Without evidence to show what happened when the brain became ill, doctors were left with few ways to treat people who struggled with symptoms of what we would now define as anxiety disorders. These individuals were institutionalized (often for life) because they could not be effectively treated for their debilitating symptoms, were sometimes in danger of harming themselves, or were a burden upon others who had to take care of them.

The symptoms of anxiety disorders look similar to what happens when someone worries. With no way of knowing it wasn't just worry, family members, clergy, and even doctors prescribed "stronger faith," "stop it," and "just think about something else" as the antidote for this "failing." To have anxiety you couldn't "just stop" was a stigma that caused individuals to be ostracized, deemed morally defective, and even institutionalized.

While our understanding of the human brain has improved considerably, the stigma of having a mental illness has not receded at the same rate with which our knowledge has expanded. Many individuals continue to feel ashamed of their illness and attempt to hide it for fear of being judged as flawed individuals with flawed faith. Hiding prohibits them from getting the very treatment needed to live a healthy life—spiritually, emotionally, and physically.

The medical term *disorder* is used to describe this grouping of illnesses and indicates the presence of a pattern of disruptions in how the body normally functions. This means anxiety disorders are illnesses characterized by specific ways in which the body malfunctions. Like any medical disorder, there are things that make an anxiety disorder better or worse, but it is not caused by moral failing or lack of willpower. Anxiety disorders are medical illnesses just like diabetes, cardiac arrhythmia, and arthritis—an important fact that has long gone misunderstood.

Anxiety disorders can be thought of in three different groups: reactions to something specific, reactions to trauma, and general or without a specific trigger. These are not scientific groups but they provide a framework for this conversation.

Anxiety Disorders Triggered by Something Specific

The American Psychological Association identifies the criteria used to diagnose mental illnesses, and four diagnoses for anxiety fit into the category of being a reaction to something specific.

Social Anxiety Disorder

Social anxiety disorder is connected to being in social settings and may be related to a specific social setting or to all social settings. Individuals suffering from this disorder want to be in social situations, but their fear is so intense they avoid them. Individuals struggling with social anxiety disorder experience:

- fear of social or performance situations where there are unfamiliar people or where they feel they could potentially act in an embarrassing manner
- intense anxiety when they are placed in social situations or need to perform

This anxiety may be so intense it creates panic attacks.[6]

Specific Phobias

Specific phobias develop as a reaction to something such as blood or spiders. Someone struggling with this disorder experiences:

- an intense, unreasonable fear either when they are in the presence of the object or anticipate they might be in the presence of the object
- intense anxiety that can even create panic attacks when they are in the presence of the object
- an awareness their fear is unreasonable but an inability to lessen the fear or change how they experience being in the presence of the object[7]

Obsessive-Compulsive Disorder

Individuals struggling with obsessive-compulsive disorder (OCD) experience intrusive thoughts about something specific such as becoming contaminated by germs or harming someone. The intrusive thoughts are highly anxiety provoking and distressing, so rituals are performed in an attempt to manage the thoughts and the anxiety they produce. These individuals often attempt to hide their rituals from others, causing them to isolate in unhealthy ways. Individuals with OCD experience:

- intrusive thoughts that are not just an extension of normal worries and are highly distressing (*My hands are contaminated and will make me sick.*)
- an inability to ignore or suppress the thoughts unless they engage in some sort of ritualistic behavior (known as a *compulsion*)
- a drive to perform the compulsion to either calm the anxiety of the thought or make sure the thought doesn't actually occur (*I must wash my hands five times without touching anything so they are no longer contaminated.*)
- an inability to stop the thoughts even though they know the thoughts and rituals are beyond what is appropriate. If they attempt to stop the thoughts or rituals, the anxiety this produces feels unbearable, so they often resume the rituals to lessen the anxiety.[8]

Agoraphobia

Individuals with agoraphobia fear being in places where it might be difficult or embarrassing to leave. The fear associated with this can become so intense individuals become unable to leave their homes. Individuals with agoraphobia avoid situations or require someone to go with them as a companion to help them face the fear.[9]

Anxiety Disorders Triggered by Trauma

Trauma reactions occur when someone experiences or is exposed to a situation that feels traumatic. It is important to recognize that what may feel traumatic to one individual may not to another. Also, what is experienced as traumatic for a child is much different than what is experienced as traumatic for an adult. For example, a child may watch a horror movie and experience it as trauma while an adult would know it is not real and would not be traumatized. Similarly, two adults may be in similar car accidents and one experiences it as trauma while the other is not particularly bothered by it. Many factors play a role in determining whether something will be experienced as trauma, including the number of previous traumas the individual has experienced. Two anxiety disorders are directly related to trauma.

Acute Stress Disorder

When an individual is exposed to a traumatic event that involves death or serious injury of some sort, they may develop an acute stress disorder where they reexperience the event repeatedly after it has passed and, within the first four weeks, experience:

- intrusive memories of the event, including distressing dreams of the event
- feeling as if the event is recurring, having flashbacks, or reliving the event
- intense distress when exposed to things connected to the event
- avoiding thoughts, feelings, activities, places, or people connected to the event
- difficulty sleeping, increased irritability, and/or difficulty concentrating

- being "on alert" all the time, resulting in hypervigilance and/or an exaggerated startle response[10]

Post-Traumatic Stress Disorder

The difference between acute stress disorder and post-traumatic stress disorder is primarily the length of time symptoms are experienced. A diagnosis of acute stress disorder applies if symptoms occur within the first four weeks after the event occurs and resolve within the same one-month period. Post-traumatic stress disorder (PTSD) is the diagnosis for these same symptoms if the event occurred over a month ago and the symptoms persist. Someone with PTSD may experience a sense of detachment from themselves, their surroundings, or their emotions—especially when reexperiencing the traumatic event or encountering something connected to the event.[11]

Anxiety Disorders without a Specific Trigger

Two anxiety disorders are not triggered by an object or experience and are more pervasive and unpredictable as a result.

Panic Attacks

A panic attack is a period of intense fear that develops seemingly out of nowhere and causes the individual to experience:

- chest pain, palpitations, or tachycardia
- chills, hot flashes, or sweating
- disconnection from reality or from themselves
- fear of losing control
- dizziness, light-headedness, or faintness
- feelings of choking, shortness of breath, or feelings of smothering
- trembling or shaking[12]

These symptoms peak within ten minutes and then slowly dissipate. The symptoms are intensely distressing, and often individuals struggling with these symptoms believe they are dying or having a heart attack.

Generalized Anxiety Disorder

Unlike individuals with specific phobias where something identifiable creates anxiety, individuals with a generalized anxiety disorder are simply anxious about many things, most of the time, for a long period of time. They find it difficult, and sometimes impossible, to control their fears and find themselves worrying and feeling:

- restless, keyed up, or on edge
- easily fatigued
- unable to concentrate or struggling to keep their mind from going blank
- irritable
- muscle tension they cannot control
- unable to get to sleep or stay asleep[13]

Individuals struggling with any of the anxiety disorders discussed above know their fear is unrealistic but cannot make it stop. The fear is so intense it interferes with their ability to function in healthy ways at work, at home, or in relationships.

Anxiety exists along a continuum from healthy anxiety to debilitating illness. While I am not a fan of self-diagnosis, it can be helpful to evaluate where you believe you fall on the continuum.

If you look back over the last year of your life and find most of the times you were anxious related to external events, the anxiety did not interfere with your ability to function in healthy ways, and the anxiety dissipated when the event passed then most of your anxiety was probably within the healthy range.

You might conclude you fall into the worry zone if you look back over the last year and find it filled with anticipation of potential problems or negative events and attempts to create plans for how to deal with all the things that might go wrong—even when you would have rather been sleeping or enjoying other activities. Worry exists on a continuum from mildly annoying to interfering with your ability to live life in the way you want to.

For some individuals, you read about the various anxiety disorders and found yourself repeatedly saying "I do this." Please know this doesn't necessarily mean you have an anxiety disorder. Instead, I would suggest it indicates you might want to explore what this means with your doctor, a counselor, or a psychiatrist as these people are trained to diagnose and treat anxiety disorders. It is important to seek assistance in determining what is happening because anxiety disorders have symptoms similar to other medical conditions, so it is vital to accurately determine what is causing the symptoms.

Whether you identified yourself as having healthy anxiety or found yourself wondering if you have an anxiety disorder, the rest of this book will help you understand both what causes you to feel anxious and what things you can do to help manage the anxiety you feel.

CHAPTER TWO

WHAT CAUSES ANXIETY?

Worry as well as anxiety disorders have many different factors that influence if they develop, when they develop, and how they are best treated. Our understanding of the factors influencing the development and treatment of mental illnesses is less advanced than for most other illnesses. Health-care systems are just beginning to understand the different factors that influence the development of illnesses and what factors must be included in any effective treatment. In this chapter, we will explore a holistic way of looking at factors that contribute to the development of worry and anxiety.

In the parable of the blind men and the elephant, a group of blind men encounter a new animal called an elephant. Being curious, they approach the animal and begin describing what they find. The first man describes the elephant as a thick snake, having felt its trunk. The second argues the elephant is some sort of fan, having experienced its ears flapping back and forth. The third groped the elephant's leg and insists it is a pillar. Another man felt along the elephant's side and insists he has encountered a wall.

The fifth man felt the tail and describes the elephant as a rope, while the last of the men felt the elephant's tusk and believes the elephant is a spear. Six men have six different experiences and, thus, six different understandings of what an elephant is. None of them are totally right, and none of them are totally wrong.[1]

The parable makes the obvious point that we tend to draw conclusions and make predictions based upon our experiences because we assume our experiences represent the totality of what is real. Most of us can think of times when we have done this and it has not gone well, but somehow this doesn't stop us from continuing to make assumptions based upon experience.

Part of the reason we do this is because our brains are "meaning making" organs. The brain takes in literally thousands of pieces of data at any given moment and makes meaning of this data by looking for recognizable patterns. When the data doesn't fit a recognizable pattern, our brain attempts to impose familiar patterns onto the data in an effort to make a familiar pattern appear. For example, what do you see when you first glance at the picture below?

Most people immediately see a triangle. However, what is actually printed on the page are three black partial circles. Our brain

fills in what isn't there to create an understanding of the picture. This sort of linear, reductionistic thinking has led to the utilization of principles like Occam's Razor. William of Ockham (or Occam) was an English philosopher and theologian in the 1300s who is credited with creating the problem-solving principle known as Occam's Razor. This principle assumes the simplest solution to a problem tends to be the right solution. Occam's Razor has been applied to most areas of life, including theology, medicine, and science.

Linear Reductionism

Our brains (and our culture as a whole) crave simplistic explanations for why something has happened and simplistic "cures" to make everything okay again. We want to know the exact cause of bad things—be they cancer, divorce, or financial hardship—so we can be sure to avoid whatever caused these bad things. If we can avoid things that cause negative experiences, we then feel in control of our lives and our future. If only life were that simple!

Occam's Razor and other similar theories have caused doctors to look at biology for the "cause" and medications for the "cure." They have caused religious leaders to look at sin or lack of faith as the "cause" and trust or increased faith as the "cure." Counselors who engage in similar thinking look at the environment you grew up in or the way you think about yourself and the world around you as the "cause" and correcting problems in thought processes or your social environment as the "cure." Much like the blind men in the parable, each of these views contains a piece of the puzzle but none of them provide complete explanations.

Systems Theory

As research has expanded to show connections between health and a broad variety of factors, the linear, reductionist theories for what "causes" and "cures" illnesses are being replaced by another idea: systems theory. A system is composed of interrelated and interdependent parts. For example, your digestive system is composed of all the different organs involved in eating, digesting, and eliminating food.

Your life is composed of all your internal systems and all the external systems you are part of. You are probably part of a family, a work environment, a faith community, a neighborhood, and so on. Each of these systems is intricately connected to you, and you are intricately connected to each of them. Each system is simultaneously *independent* (because it performs its own unique set of functions) and *interdependent* (because every system is surrounded by and influenced by other systems). Systems theory assumes that when you change one part of any system, it affects other parts of the same system and all other systems it is associated with. Researchers utilizing systems theory want to understand not only how each system functions internally but also how different systems influence one another. Systems theory assumes biological, psychological, social, and spiritual systems all contribute to the development of illnesses and need to be part of any effective, holistic treatment for illness. Let's look at each system separately first.

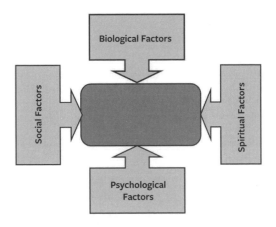

Biological Factors

Until recently, if your annual physical showed your blood sugar to be high, your doctor would diagnose you as having diabetes. The doctor would explain that your pancreas was no longer functioning normally so you would need to give yourself injections of insulin and limit your carbohydrate intake to manage your blood sugar. While this simple explanation correctly identifies someone who is diabetic as having an abnormally functioning pancreas, it fails to identify all the different factors that both contribute to the development of diabetes and will need to be addressed in order to appropriately manage the illness.

Organizations like the Centers for Disease Control (CDC) have done extensive research to help identify factors that influence who will develop certain illnesses and how the illness will affect their lives. For example, research clearly shows genetic predisposition plays a role in determining whether an individual will develop diabetes. However, we also know weight, diet, exercise, and the overall health of an individual also influence both the development of diabetes and how the illness progresses.

Similarly, heredity has been shown to impact whether an individual will develop an anxiety disorder. Diet, exercise, and other health conditions have also been shown to impact both the development of an anxiety disorder and its ability to be treated effectively.

Psychological Factors

Substantial research has been conducted on the connection between the mind and the body. This research has shown that chronic stress affects the immune system and creates issues within the gastrointestinal system. As the body of research expands, the impact of our thought patterns on our health is becoming clearer. A study conducted in 2014 showed cynicism is connected to an increased risk of developing dementia.[2] Another study looked at one hundred thousand women and found the more cynical the women were, the more likely they were to develop heart disease.[3] How you think about yourself and those around you impacts both the illnesses you will develop and how you will deal with those illnesses.

Both worry and anxiety disorders are profoundly affected by how you think about yourself and the world around you. Worry is created and controlled by our thought patterns. Anxiety disorders can also be exacerbated by thought patterns, and thought patterns can have a profound impact upon their treatment.

Social Factors

Recently, our understanding of factors contributing to the development of illnesses has expanded to include variables called social determinants of health. The CDC has researched and can clearly show that conditions in your environment affect your health. Living in a safe neighborhood, being able to afford to buy healthy foods, and having a good education are predictive of both which illnesses you may develop and how those illnesses will progress.[4]

An individual living in an inner city with a minimum wage job has fewer resources available and is more likely to both develop illnesses and have difficulty managing them once they develop.

The environment within which you were raised and currently live impacts the development of anxiety disorders as well as the amount of worry you find yourself experiencing. If you live in a safe neighborhood with good resources, you have less need to worry about the basic necessities of life than if you live fearing a drive-by shooting or wondering if you will have enough food to feed your family for the week. Living with consistent stressors in your environment can contribute to the development of anxiety disorders and may also impact your ability to successfully cope with an anxiety disorder if one develops.

Spiritual Factors

Spirituality and health were linked to one another from the beginning of recorded history until the late seventeenth century, when the Enlightenment movement began, and remain linked in many developing nations. Prior to the Enlightenment, physicians were often clergy. Religious institutions were responsible for licensing physicians to practice medicine and for building and staffing hospitals to treat the ill. During the Enlightenment, however, reason came to be identified as valid while tradition, feeling, and faith were treated with suspicion and regarded as crutches utilized by the uneducated. The intricate connection between faith and medicine sometimes led to horrendous practices such as performing exorcisms to treat conditions like epilepsy. However, completely separating faith from medicine created problems that have been just as devastating.

As the research examining the influence of religion and spirituality on health has expanded, faith is consistently proving to be an important part of both the prevention and treatment of illness—including anxiety. Studies have shown people with regular spiritual practices tend to live longer[5] and have lower levels of chemicals within the body linked to disease development.[6] In addition to helping prevent illness, faith has been shown to positively impact how individuals who become ill cope with their illness and recover.[7] An individual's belief in God also affects the amount of anxiety they experience when coping with mistakes they make. Studies show people who believe in God and think about God when they are in stressful situations or make mistakes physiologically experience lower levels of anxiety and report feeling calmer than atheists under the same circumstances.[8]

Systems Theory and Anxiety

Biology, thoughts, feelings, social environment, and spiritual factors all influence whether someone will struggle with worry or an anxiety disorder. These same components must be integrated into any healthy plan for addressing worry and anxiety disorders. The next several chapters will look at how each of these factors contributes to both worry and anxiety disorders as well as how they can be leveraged as part of an effective treatment for both worry and anxiety disorders.

CHAPTER THREE

BIOLOGY AFFECTS ANXIETY

I frequently joked with my kids during their growing-up years that their teeth were their dad's fault. My family historically has good teeth—my mother didn't have cavities, and neither do my siblings or I. My husband was not so lucky! He passed this on to our children to the point I used to joke with my teenage daughter that her mouth was worth more than my car (which it literally was). While my children's genetic code caused their teeth to form in ways that left them vulnerable to cavities, the food they ate and the ways in which they cared for their teeth also played a role in the health of their teeth. While brushing and flossing daily and avoiding sugary snacks didn't totally prevent cavities, it did impact how many they developed and how fast those cavities grew. The same is true with anxiety disorders.

Many biological factors influence whether we will develop an anxiety disorder—some of which we understand and some of which we are just beginning to learn about. As with many illnesses, we can't accurately predict who will and who won't develop an anxiety disorder, just what factors seem to contribute to its development, and what factors will help to effectively treat anxiety once it has developed. While we do not know exactly what causes some individuals to develop an anxiety disorder, we do know biological changes occur within the body when someone has an anxiety disorder. These changes often require medical intervention in order to effectively manage the disorder. Just like diabetes is a disorder created by a chemical imbalance within the body, there is a great deal of evidence that anxiety disorders also occur because of chemical imbalances within the body.

When someone develops diabetes, it is important to look at what medications are needed to effectively treat the illness as well as address issues within the individual's lifestyle, diet, and exercise, as these are also important components of effective treatment. The same is also true of an anxiety disorder. In this chapter we will look at how heredity, chemical imbalances, age, and other medical conditions contribute to anxiety and identify steps that can be taken to effectively treat the biological components of anxiety.

Biological Factors Contributing to Anxiety

Heredity

Sometimes a family system seems littered with individuals who have anxiety disorders while at other times one individual within the family system has an anxiety disorder and no one else does. Unlike characteristics like eye color or illnesses like cystic fibrosis, there is no one gene we can clearly link to the development of an anxiety disorder. While this is true, it doesn't mean heredity plays no role. Sometimes anxiety disorders develop as a result of what is called multifactorial inheritance. Multifactorial inheritance refers to a combination of environmental factors and mutations within multiple genes that, together, seem to cause an illness or disease to develop. Multifactorial inheritance means no one gene has the power to determine whether a person develops an anxiety disorder. Instead, a number of small mutations in different genes create a susceptibility to the illness. When someone with this susceptibility encounters environmental factors that push up against this area of genetic weakness, the illness develops as a result.

Chemical Imbalances

Regardless of whether heredity is involved in the development of an anxiety disorder, individuals who develop anxiety disorders appear to have abnormalities in the chemical systems within their body. Abnormalities in as many as ten different brain systems may be linked to the development of panic disorders.[1] In particular, scientists have looked at how certain chemicals called neurotransmitters, which act as messengers within the brain and central nervous system, affect anxiety.

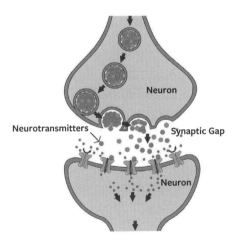

The structures of the brain and central nervous system are made up of neurons. These neurons sit close to one another but do not touch. The space between them is called the synaptic gap. Neurotransmitters carry messages from the neurons of one cell to the neurons in the next by traveling across this synaptic gap. If, for any reason, there are not enough of these neurotransmitters or they are prevented from traveling from one neuron to the next, the result is a mental illness like anxiety or depression.

One group of neurotransmitters that appear to be linked to anxiety disorders includes serotonin, norepinephrine, and dopamine. All three of these neurotransmitters play essential roles in maintaining a healthy mood. When individuals struggling with anxiety disorders are given antidepressants to increase the amount of these neurotransmitters available for the body to use, their symptoms of anxiety can often be effectively managed.[2] Antidepressants are often considered the treatment of choice for anxiety disorders but, like any medications, have side effects, and not everyone finds them to be effective. Additionally, antidepressants take four to six weeks to begin working and often must be gradually increased to reach an effective dose. This can leave individuals struggling with anxiety for a significant period of time after they seek treatment.

Another neurotransmitter called gamma-aminobutyric acid (GABA) is involved in controlling the body's response to stress. GABA binds itself to neurons within the nervous system and calms them.[3] Several studies have shown individuals who have panic disorders also have lower levels of GABA than control groups without a history of panic disorders.[4] Medications called benzodiazepines can be utilized to enhance the effects of GABA because they bind to the same places where GABA would normally bind.[5] While these medications rapidly calm the body and alleviate anxiety, they are addictive, sedating, and their effects typically only last four to six hours.[6]

Understanding chemical imbalances that play a role in the development of anxiety disorders makes it important for those struggling with an anxiety disorder to seek medical treatment. Medication is sometimes needed to effectively manage the symptoms.

Age

Age, in and of itself, does not cause anxiety. Anxiety disorders can, and do, develop in young children, but they can also develop as we age. Around 50 percent of people who develop a generalized anxiety disorder do so later in life.[7] Women appear to have an increased risk of developing anxiety disorders later in life compared to their male counterparts.[8] There is some evidence the hormonal changes during and after menopause may increase vulnerability to anxiety disorders for women who had not previously struggled with anxiety.[9] The human brain, like all systems within the body, both slows and is more prone to problems as we age. This, combined with the increased likelihood of developing other medical conditions, can contribute to the development of anxiety disorders.

Illness

Being diagnosed with a chronic illness brings huge changes to an individual's body and life. Everything about their world is touched by learning to live with a chronic condition. Frequently, symptoms need to be monitored to both control the illness and make sure it is not progressing. Additionally, the individual can no longer live believing "nothing bad will happen to me," because something bad has happened. This makes it easy to become fixated on what else might go wrong and to begin obsessively worrying. A chronic illness also causes increased stress on the body as the body works to continue doing everything necessary despite the illness. This ongoing stress can gradually deplete the body of the neurotransmitters essential for managing both depression and anxiety.

Some illnesses and their treatments also contribute to the development of anxiety disorders. The Mayo Clinic reports heart disease, diabetes, hyperthyroidism, chronic obstructive pulmonary disease, and irritable bowel syndrome can all contribute to the development of anxiety disorders.[10] Additionally, many of these illnesses require medication to effectively manage them. All medications have side effects, and sometimes these effects include anxiety.

Substance Use/Abuse

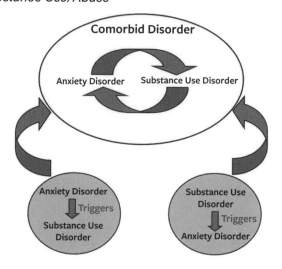

"Decades of research in psychiatry have shown that anxiety disorders and substance use disorders co-occur at greater rates than would be expected by chance alone."[11] Individuals with generalized anxiety disorder or panic disorder are at the highest risk of also having a substance use disorder.[12] Individuals with obsessive-compulsive disorder or post-traumatic stress disorder are at increased risk of having alcohol-related disorders, but not other drug-related disorders.[13] Substance use disorders and anxiety disorders are considered *comorbid*; they often coexist, with one feeding into the other. As the figure above shows, substance use can sometimes trigger the development of an anxiety disorder. This is not as common as when anxiety disorders lead to the development of substance use disorders. About 75 percent of the time, anxiety disorders exist before the substance use disorder develops.[14] This appears to be connected to the fact that individuals struggling with anxiety disorders experience incredible distress and often attempt to manage this by self-medicating instead of seeking medical attention. The businessperson struggling with anxiety who has a drink to "take the edge off" or the college student who smokes a joint to help them relax and not care so much about whether they pass or fail the test are both attempting to "medicate" their worry or anxiety. While self-medicating may seem effective in the moment, it doesn't truly address the underlying anxiety disorder and leads to increased use and dependency over time. Additionally, having a substance use disorder makes treatment of anxiety disorders more difficult. The comorbidity increases the difficulty of successfully treating the anxiety disorder and is also associated with higher rates of the anxiety disorder reoccurring after it has been successfully treated.[15] Individuals who have both a panic disorder and a substance use disorder are also at increased risk for death by suicide when compared to individuals who have a panic disorder with no substance use disorder.[16] So, while anxiety disorders are only sometimes caused by substance use, it is important to be aware of the comorbidity of these two disorders. It is easy to begin using substances in an attempt to manage the symptoms of the anxiety disorder and inadvertently create an additional illness which must then be addressed.

Steps to Manage Biological Causes of Anxiety

The list of potential biological factors contributing to anxiety disorders discussed in this chapter is by no means exhaustive. It is imperative that individuals experiencing anxiety seek medical attention to accurately assess what is causing the symptoms they are experiencing and what will be needed to effectively treat those symptoms. Many individuals who would not hesitate to seek medical assistance if they identified a lump in their breast or a rash over their torso resist going to the doctor when they begin experiencing symptoms of anxiety. Because mental illnesses continue to be stigmatized, individuals are reticent to seek treatment until the illness has progressed to the point they can no longer function. When medical intervention occurs early in the progression of the illness, it minimizes the impact of the illness on overall functioning and allows symptoms to be more easily brought under control. In addition to seeking medical treatment, it is also important to address other aspects of your life as your body's physical health is affected by the food you eat, the stress in your life, the way you think, your sleep patterns, and how much you exercise.

Medication

Just like blood pressure medications regulate a system within the body, medication can be used to regulate the systems of the body creating anxiety. However, unlike with blood pressure medications, people have many misconceptions about medications used to treat mental health issues. Some common myths include:

> *"Medication is just a crutch."* The medication is simply correcting a chemical imbalance within the brain and allowing your body to function the way it was created. We take medication to balance our blood pressure, blood sugar levels, thyroid function, and many other systems within the body and would never call those a crutch. The medication is doing work you cannot do for yourself. This, in turn, gives you the ability to do the work (like learning to think differently) you can do yourself. Medication alone is rarely

the solution to an anxiety disorder. However, it is often an important part of the treatment.

"I don't want to take pills so I can feel normal. I don't want to take something that might change my personality." Medications used to treat anxiety disorders don't stop you from feeling what you would normally feel and they don't change your personality. They are designed to manage the anxious feelings, not to stop you from experiencing your life as you normally would.

"If I start to take medication, I will be stuck on it for life." Most individuals take medication to treat anxiety disorders for a period of time but do not need to take it for a lifetime. For a small number of individuals, their body consistently does not produce enough of the chemicals needed to manage anxiety effectively and they will need to take medication consistently throughout their life to remain healthy. However, this is not the experience of most people.

Unfortunately, treating disorders that affect the brain isn't as simple as running a blood test to identify how low your iron count is or testing your blood sugar to know how much insulin to prescribe. While all brains are structured in the same fashion, each one responds uniquely to medication. It is essential for you to work closely with a doctor you trust and to remember this will be a process. Finding an effective medication requires trying a prescription, noting what does and does not work, and adjusting based upon this information. You will need to communicate regularly with your doctor about the symptoms that are improving and those that continue to cause difficulty so they can make adjustments. Treating anxiety with medication often requires trying several different medications before identifying one that works well for you.

Physicians utilize three major groupings of medication to help treat anxiety.

Antidepressants

Antidepressants work to increase the amount of various neurotransmitters available within the synaptic gap by signaling the brain not to reabsorb them. This allows the brain to function as it was designed. These medications are not habit forming but, since the brain is an incredibly sensitive organ, they must be started at low doses and slowly increased as the brain adjusts. It often takes four to six weeks for the medications to start to be effective. Once the medication starts to become effective, it is important to continue working with your physician until a dosage is found that manages the symptoms effectively. It is also important to communicate any side effects you experience to your doctor. When your symptoms have been managed, it is important to stay on the medication for between six and twelve months while your brain has a chance to replenish its supply of neurotransmitters to have enough available when you go off the medication. Antidepressants must also be discontinued very slowly to minimize their impact upon the body, so it is important not to just stop taking them.

Benzodiazepines

Unlike antidepressants, which are not addictive, benzodiazepines are addictive. They are also highly effective in managing the symptoms of anxiety on a short-term basis. These medications work like neurotransmitters and bind to the neurons in a way that calms the neural activity. They have an effect on the body similar to swaddling a distressed infant to help them calm down. Physicians often use these medications in combination with an antidepressant for the first few weeks to give the antidepressant time to become effective. These medications can also be used as "rescue medications" taken only when experiencing uncontrollable symptoms of anxiety. For example, an individual experiencing a panic attack can take a benzodiazepine to help stop the attack. If these medications are taken consistently for several months, they should only be discontinued under the supervision of a physician; abrupt withdrawal can lead to agitation, irritation, seizures, vomiting, muscle cramps, and sweating.

Beta Blockers

Beta blockers work to interrupt the body's fight or flight response by blocking adrenaline and noradrenaline. Adrenaline and noradrenaline are the hormones the body releases when it perceives danger to prepare the muscles for action. Suppressing the release of these hormones slows the body's fight or flight response. These medications are also used to treat high blood pressure, angina, and migraines. While these medications are not habit forming, they do lower blood pressure, making it important for your doctor to monitor your blood pressure to be sure it remains in a healthy range as you start them.

Caffeine

Caffeine is the drug of choice for many of us . . . we start our morning with it and find ourselves going back for more every time our cup runs dry throughout the day. However, our "pick me up" can also contribute to anxiety. Caffeine is a stimulant. It stimulates the body by causing it to release more of the hormone noradrenaline. Noradrenaline is one of the chemicals released when the body perceives danger and kicks into fight or flight. Caffeine affects noradrenaline for everyone who ingests it, but individuals who have anxiety disorders appear to be more sensitive to these effects.[17] Caffeine may not cause your anxiety but it does contribute to anxiety. It also has a six-hour half-life. This means six hours after you drink it, half of the caffeine is still in your system. So, limiting caffeine intake can be an important part of managing an anxiety disorder.

Diet

When we are not feeling well, we tend to be drawn to comfort foods—foods that are high in sugar and fat. While these foods are attractive to us in the moment, they may also contribute to higher levels of anxiety and depression.[18] This negative feedback loop seems to be part of the explanation for why individuals struggling with anxiety and depression tend to have diets low in fruits and vegetables and high in fats and sugars.[19] Instead of reaching for comfort foods, creating a diet rich in complex carbohydrates, omega fatty acids, and adequate water will be more effective in helping you to feel less anxious. Such a diet also has the added side effect of helping you to be healthier overall.

Simple carbohydrates, like those found in processed foods and foods high in sugar, contribute to blood sugar spikes and lows that can create a jittery feeling. Complex carbohydrates, on the other hand, are digested more slowly, resulting in more stable blood sugar levels. Stable blood sugars can help your body feel calmer. Similarly, omega fatty acids have been linked to improving symptoms of both depression and anxiety.[20]

Zinc and magnesium have both been found to lower anxiety levels.[21] Zinc can be found in oysters, cashews, beef, and eggs. Green leafy vegetables like spinach as well as nuts, whole grains, and legumes are good sources for magnesium.

Adjusting your diet is not a substitute for seeking medical attention when you are experiencing symptoms of an anxiety disorder. However, there is an increasing amount of research showing there is a relationship between what you eat and the anxiety you experience. Based upon this, modifying your diet *as well as* seeking medical treatment may help you to effectively manage anxiety.

Exercise

When you are experiencing anxiety, exercise is usually the last thing on your mind. However, exercise has been proven to have a positive impact on anxiety disorders in numerous studies.[22] Both high- and low-intensity aerobic exercises have been shown to reduce anxiety, so you don't have to run competitively in order to benefit from the effects of exercise. The key appears to be engaging in aerobic exercise that uses large muscle groups for between fifteen and thirty minutes at least three times per week. Aerobic exercise is activity that raises your heart rate into its target range and holds it there consistently. You could consider walking, swimming, water aerobics, jogging, or cycling, as these are all aerobic exercises. If the thought of exercising for fifteen minutes feels daunting, consider starting with just five minutes and building up. Don't pick an exercise that feels like torture, because this won't be sustainable. Instead, pick something you think you might enjoy and begin slowly. If you are an extrovert, consider joining a class or exercising with a friend. If you are more introverted, you might want to find an online aerobic routine you can do in your basement where no one is watching and you don't have to talk to anyone. After you have consulted with your physician to be sure your body is healthy enough to engage in aerobic exercise, pick something that feels attainable and find a way to sustain it over time.

Breathing

In the first chapter, we looked at what happens when your body is stressed and the fight or flight response activates. While many of the ways the body responds when it kicks into fight or flight are not things we have any control over—like our heart rate—our breathing is one thing we do have the ability to control. Research shows individuals with anxiety disorders take over fifteen breaths per minute. Conversely, individuals without anxiety disorders take closer to twelve.[23] Working to manage your breathing is one way you can intervene in the fight or flight response and effectively short-circuit the pattern.

Managing your breathing takes deliberate practice over time so that, when you are experiencing increased anxiety, you can utilize the skill. The type of breathing you need to learn is called diaphragmatic breathing. To do this:

- Sit comfortably.
- Place a hand on your stomach.
- Begin by breathing in over a count of five at a rate of about one count per second. Gently breathe in through your nose. As you breathe in, your stomach should expand outward and your shoulders should not lift.
- Hold the breath for a count of two.
- Gently exhale through your mouth over a count of six.
- Rest for a count of two.
- Repeat this ten times.

If you find yourself off count or feeling out of breath, relax and start again. Don't try to force yourself to breathe deeply, just let your lungs naturally fill with air. Be sure to limit the stimulation around you to help you focus better. You can practice this anywhere—at your desk, taking a slow walk (one count per step), lying in bed, and even while going to the bathroom (okay, maybe not for the full ten repetitions). Slowing your breathing will eventually slow your heart rate, which, in turn, begins to calm your body. By practicing this exercise several times throughout your day, it will become second nature and you will be able to readily access this skill when you feel yourself beginning to become more anxious.

Progressive Relaxation

Progressive relaxation was developed by Dr. Edmund Jacobson in the 1920s. He was a physician who recognized many of his patients' complaints about aches and pains appeared to be connected to muscle tension they didn't know how to release. He developed a series of exercises to help his patients learn to release this tension. This technique has since been studied extensively in relationship to anxiety and shown to effectively lower anxiety levels. Progressive relaxation can be done anywhere, without anyone being aware you are doing it. Follow these steps:

- Sit comfortably, or lie down if it is easier.
- Start with your feet. Tighten every part of one foot as tightly as you can get it and hold it in that position for a count of five.
- Release all the tension and allow your foot to totally relax. Be aware of the feel of your foot now that it is relaxed.
- Repeat this activity with the other foot.
- Gradually work up your body, tensing each muscle group, holding it for a count of five, and then releasing all the tension and being aware of how relaxed it feels.
- When you get to the top of your head, you can either conclude the exercise or start with your feet again if you continue to feel anxious.

This exercise, like the breathing exercise, must be practiced so it becomes familiar enough that you can remember how to do it when you are feeling anxiety. Also, each time you practice you lower your anxiety. Doing this even two times a day will lower your anxiety at least slightly during the day.

Mitigating Biological Factors Affecting Anxiety

Reading about all the ways our biology may be stacked against us can feel defeating and anxiety provoking. Many of the things talked about in this chapter are not under our control. However, there are still steps we can take to effectively care for our bodies and minimize the impact of our biology on anxiety.

An illustration I use to help both myself and my clients is related to a car I inherited as a young adult. When my grandmother passed away, she had a very ugly brown car she had literally only driven to church and back for many years. It was older and it was big, but it was in good condition. I was poor and in need of reliable transportation, so my parents graciously gifted me this car. I didn't get to choose the color, the size, or the design—I inherited it, and it was effective in getting me from point to point for many years. While I didn't get to choose the car, I did get to choose how I cared for it. I could perform the routine maintenance so it would remain reliable and last for a long time, or neglect it and allow it to fall apart because it wasn't exactly what I would have chosen. The same is true of our bodies. God gifts us—through our parents—with bodies (vehicles) that house our spirits while we are here on this earth. These bodies are designed to allow us to co-labor with him and be vessels of his love while we are here. We didn't get to choose these bodies, they contain flaws created by living in a fallen world, and they may not be what we wish they were in many ways. However, just like I had to choose whether I was going to take care of my ugly, brown granny-mobile, we each face a choice about how we will care for the bodies God has given us. Our choices help determine how smoothly our bodies run and how long they last before they start to experience mechanical issues.

Below is a list of action steps you might consider implementing as ways to regularly take better care of your body. Please, don't attempt to do all these activities at once. Pick one to start with and consistently work at this activity for at least twenty-one days before adding another activity. Effective, lasting change takes time, and new habits take at least twenty-one days to form.

- If you have not had a physical in the last year, schedule an appointment with your primary care physician to have a complete physical. If you have been experiencing symptoms of anxiety, make a list of these symptoms and consider discussing them with your physician. If you are hesitant to do this, remember there are illnesses that can create or mimic symptoms of anxiety. It is important to your overall health for you to give your doctor all the information you can so they can effectively care for you.

- Keep a record of how much caffeine you take in each day for a week. If you are consuming more than the equivalent of one or two cups of coffee, consider cutting back or eliminating caffeine altogether. If you are consuming caffeine within six hours of your normal bedtime, remember caffeine has a six-hour half-life. You will sleep better if you stop drinking caffeine at least six hours before bedtime.

- Keep a record of your food intake for a week and then go through the record and circle all the high sugar, high fat, and processed foods you consumed. Look for patterns around when you tend to eat those types of foods and pick one thing you could do to increase your consumption of complex carbohydrates, omega fatty acids, or water. Work to make this one change in your diet consistently for at least twenty-one days. When you reach the twenty-one-day mark, keep a record of your food intake for a week and compare it to the first log. Make sure to give yourself credit for progress toward your goal and then consider what you would like to do next to move yourself toward a healthier diet.

- Pick a way you would like to increase the amount of exercise in your daily life. Remember to start small, and if you have not had a physical in the last year, it is important to do this prior to starting any new exercise program! After you have picked what you would like to do, consider how you are going to motivate yourself to make this change in your life. I am competitive, so I am currently competing in a virtual "race" with my daughter and nieces to see who can cover the distance we selected first. My daughter bikes, I walk, and my nieces run. At other times in my life, I have rewarded myself with something I wanted after I had consistently exercised for a specific period of time. The important part is picking something motivating for *you*. Remember, new habits take at least twenty-one days to form, so plan to start small. Don't feel the need to increase what you are doing until you have established a pattern of being able to maintain your current activity for at least twenty-one days.
- Practice the diaphragmatic breathing exercise at least two times per day for the next twenty-one days.
- Practice the progressive relaxation exercise at least two times per day for the next twenty-one days.

CHAPTER FOUR

HOW WE THINK AND WHAT WE THINK AFFECT ANXIETY

We all enter the world as totally helpless infants who are dependent upon the adults around us to provide for all our needs. What's more, when we make our entrance into the world, we don't possess the ability to see ourselves as an individual separate from the adults in our world—particularly our mother. God created humanity so everyone would always need someone outside of themselves to tell them who they are. God is relational—the Father, Son, and Holy Spirit exist in a perfect love relationship with one another. Each member of the Trinity loves the others perfectly and receives love from the others perfectly. From this love relationship, God created Adam. God formed Adam and then spoke identity to him by naming him. Adam lived in a perfect relationship with God—he received love and identity from God and, because of this, he perfectly loved God.

God looked at his creation and declared, "It is not good for the man to be alone" (Gen. 2:18). What God had created didn't replicate what he knew to be perfect love. So God created Eve,

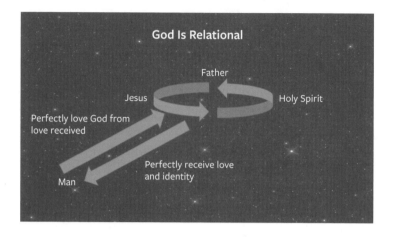

and from the perfect love Adam received from God, Adam spoke identity over Eve by naming her. Thus, a perfect representation of the Triune God's love relationship was created on earth.

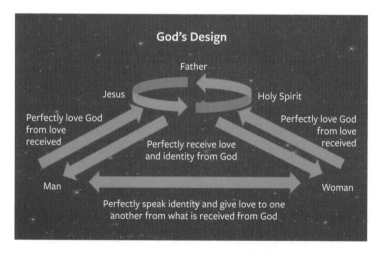

"God saw all that he had made, and it was very good" (Gen. 1:31). If only we still lived in this reality! Unfortunately, sin entered the world and, when it did, it brought death—death to our perfect ability to give and receive both love and identity. We now live in a world where we are incapable of perfectly giving or receiving love and incapable of perfectly speaking identity or receiving words of identity spoken over us.

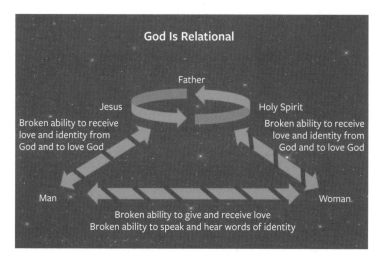

Even though our ability to receive love and words of identity has been damaged, we continue to need love and words of identity in order to be healthy individuals. This fundamental need to be in relationships where we both give and receive love and words of identity is why we form attachments.

Our first attachment is to our mother. There is a growing body of research suggesting this first attachment begins in utero.[1] Once born, our primary caregivers become the source of all our physical and emotional needs. They teach us who we are and what we can expect from the world around us. While these basic beliefs can be changed later in life and are affected by experiences throughout our lives, the "bedrock" is formed in the first years of life through our experiences and the meaning we give to these experiences.[2] Our brains encode this information and store it as memories we later draw upon in new situations. So, before we delve into what we learn and the meaning we give it, it is important to take a minute to look at the different types of memories we form and draw upon. Psychologists divide memory into two broad categories:

Implicit Memory: skills, procedures, or associations that are automatic and we don't consciously recall.[3] Examples of this include being fearful of dogs if you were bitten by a dog when you were an infant, knowing how to walk, and knowing how to tie your shoes.

Explicit Memory: facts and experiences we are consciously aware of and that require thought on our part.[4] Examples of this include learning your multiplication facts, remembering your first kiss, and knowing how to change a car tire.

Within these two main categories of memory, it can be helpful to break things down a bit more. These three types of memories can be either implicit or explicit:

Factual Memory: facts we have learned to be true, such as 2 + 2 = 4, the world is round, God is love, and so forth.[5]

Pattern Memory: stored sequences that allow us to do things. Walking is a pattern of muscle movements that happen in a certain order every time. The same can be true of things like driving a car, washing the dishes, or most anything we do repetitively.[6]

Episodic or Experiential Memory: experiences in our life that form our understanding of ourself and the world around us.[7] For example, if you ran into the open arms of your father every night when he got home from work, and he scooped you up in a giant hug and told you how amazing you were and how much he had missed you all day, this formed an experience of being adored that impacts both what you believe about all fathers and what you believe to be true about yourself.

Dividing memory into these three categories is extremely helpful, because once we have learned something, we can only replace it with a stronger memory of the same type. If I learned 2 + 2 = 5 instead of 2 + 2 = 4, the way I would replace my faulty factual memory is by learning a new replacement fact. I would repeat "2 + 2 = 4" over and over until this new fact had become stronger than the old one and "written over" the 2 + 2 = 5 fact in my brain.

The same is true of pattern memory. If I learn to pitch a softball using poor form, the coach can't teach me to do it correctly by just having me memorize the facts about how to pitch correctly. I would need to slow my original throwing pattern down and consciously learn a new pattern for throwing by repeating it over and over until it becomes strong enough and ingrained enough to replace the old sequence of muscle movements in my brain.

Moving on to experiential memory, if I learned as a child that breaking down into tears resulted in people yelling at me and hitting me until I stopped, I can't change this experience of "crying is a dangerous thing" by simply learning new facts. I could memorize the fact "crying is a normal and natural emotion that is healthy," but I am still going to experience it as something dangerous. Changing this understanding of crying would require me to have more powerful experiences of being accepted, comforted, and validated when I cry than my previous experiences of being harmed when I cried. The only things that can overwrite experiential memories are more emotionally powerful experiential memories. Think about this for a moment—no matter how many times I tell myself I am lovable, if I had intense childhood experiences of being treated as unlovable, the factual information will sit in my brain while I continue to *experience* myself as unlovable. Until my factual understanding of being lovable is coupled with powerful *experiences* of being well-loved, the original experiential memory won't be changed.

It is equally important to remember my experiential memories represent exactly that—*my* experiences. My children experienced me as "yelling" at them when I was upset with them. I found it extremely distressing when they begged me to "stop yelling" at them. See, I grew up in a family where yelling abounded, and I knew I was not doing anything of the sort. However, my children experienced my stern and direct commands to stop doing something immediately as yelling and, thus, their experience was that when they did something wrong they were yelled at. This was their experience, but it doesn't mean I was, in fact, even raising my voice. We remember our experiences, not necessarily what literally happened. Our experiences need to be treated as valid but not as a gospel account of what literally happened. My children and I still joke about when they learned what being yelled at by their mother would really sound like. In a moment of exasperation, after repeatedly attempting to prove I wasn't yelling, I took my children to the basement, made sure all the doors and windows were shut so I wouldn't alarm any neighbors, and yelled nonsense words at the top of my voice for what felt like an eternity. Their eyes became as big as saucers, and suddenly we all had a common understanding of what yelling was and was not. They had experienced yelling and now were open to exploring new language for what they experienced when I was being directive and stern.

With this as our backdrop, let's move to exploring how what we learn about ourselves and others impacts the types of attachments we form and the amount of anxiety and worry we experience.

Attachment Styles

We are born without the ability to know what is true about us as individuals and without the ability to meet our own needs. As a result, we seek connection with individuals who can fulfill these basic needs in our life. Their reactions to us and to our needs determine how we view both ourselves and the world around us. Our primary attachments teach us two things:

Am I competent and capable?

Can I depend on others to meet my needs when I am in distress?

The answers to these two questions form our pattern for attaching in relationships. The answer to the first question forms our view of ourself. The answer to the second question forms our view of others.

View of Self

If my primary caregivers give me consistent messages that they see me as able to handle age-appropriate tasks in my world, encourage me to take risks and try new things, and validate both my successes and my frustration at failure, I learn I am a competent individual who is capable of managing situations, dealing with problems, and handling failure. But what if my caregivers consistently hover over me as I try new things, anxiously attempting to ensure I never make mistakes, never try potentially risky new things, and never experience failure? While they may be well-intentioned, I learn I am not capable of handling the normal bumps and bruises of life, don't know how to make healthy decisions, and couldn't possibly survive on my own if something bad were to happen. At the other extreme, if my caregivers ridicule my imperfect childish attempts at new tasks, are angry with me when

I make mistakes while learning, and push me out of the way to do things themselves when I am not moving fast enough, they teach me this same lesson: I am not competent to handle the tasks of life.

View of Others

If, beginning in infancy, my primary caregivers consistently react to my cries for help and are generally able to comfort me and meet my needs without becoming overwhelmed themselves, I learn I can depend on them to take care of me when I have physical, emotional, and relational needs. I see others as dependable, capable, and trustworthy. When my primary caregivers attend to my needs, they successfully both calm me emotionally and reassure me I am okay—things I am currently unable to do for myself. They help regulate and manage my emotions, and their consistent ability to do this models the skills I will copy as I learn to soothe myself when they are not present.

However, if I cry out in distress and experience my cries as totally unanswered or unanswered for distressingly long periods of time, I will emotionally shut down to avoid the pain of the unmet need and will learn I can't depend upon people to care for me when I am in distress. If I cry out in distress and these cries create distress within the caregiver who responds or overwhelm their skills so they are unable to calm me and take care of what I need, I learn my needs are too much for the people around me to care for. I am left in overwhelming distress and also have no one to teach me the skills I must learn in order to regulate my emotions and calm myself when I am upset. Finally, if I cry out in distress and am punished with harsh words or actions, I learn I can't depend upon people to meet my needs and people may harm me if I have needs.

Forming Attachment Styles

From the answers to *Am I competent and capable?* and *Can I depend on others to meet my needs when I am in distress?*, researchers and theorists have identified four basic attachment styles.[8] While attachment styles do not cause anxiety, they contribute to why we might experience worry and anxiety. Identifying and modifying our basic understanding of ourselves and others so it is healthier can help us to shift how we function within our attachment styles to more effectively get our needs met and experience less worry and anxiety.

Stable Attachment Style

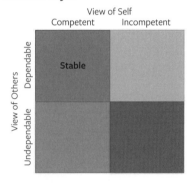

Individuals who have a stable attachment style have experiential memories that taught them they are competent individuals and others in their world can generally be relied upon to assist them when they have needs. Developing a secure attachment requires the child's primary caregivers to be aware of and consistently, appropriately responsive to the needs of the child both emotionally and physically. Caregivers who can calmly respond in an organized and effective fashion when the child's feeling of safety and security has been threatened, when the child is hungry, when the child has been ill, or when the child is upset provide the child with experiential memories that others can be trusted to consistently, appropriately meet their needs when they ask for assistance. Over time, they also learn from these caregivers how to self-soothe and regulate their emotions so they can calm themselves routinely without always needing the assistance of someone else.

Additionally, individuals who develop stable attachments have experiential memories of being encouraged by their caregivers to try new things and appropriately supported in a calm, reassuring manner as they attempt new things. When the child is unsuccessful, they are comforted, reassured, and encouraged to try again. Each little step toward mastering the new task is celebrated and reinforced by the caregiver who calmly manages their own emotions and remains encouraging throughout the process. Children with these sorts of consistent experiences encode memories of themselves as competent and capable to handle new situations, unexpected problems, and disappointments.

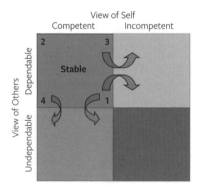

Research shows about 46 percent of the general population have a stable attachment style.[9] However, the stability of this attachment is variable and can change over the course of the individual's life. Individuals 1 and 3 from the diagram above would both have a stable attachment but a tendency to see themselves as less competent than individuals 2 and 4. When stressed, individuals 1 and 3 could move to a place of seeing themselves as incompetent. Individuals 1 and 4 have a stable attachment style but also have experiences that leave them seeing others as less dependable than individuals 2 and 3. When stressed enough, individuals 1 and 4 could move toward isolating and not sharing their needs out of a fear their needs won't be met in healthy ways.

Having a stable attachment does not preclude you from experiencing anxiety or worry. It does, however, give you a more solid sense of yourself and others from which to deal with anxiety and worry. For example, if Michaela is experiencing symptoms of acute stress disorder after having been in a near-fatal car accident, her view of herself as someone capable of handling difficult emotions and situations will influence how she talks to herself about her experience and the level of emotional distress she experiences as a result. It will also impact her skill in successfully regulating her emotions. She is more likely to know how to calm herself when she finds herself anxiously reliving the events of the accident and more likely to be able to reassure herself that, while this is currently distressing, she won't always feel this way. Her view of others as dependable and capable of responding to her needs will enable her to more easily reach out to others in the midst of her distress, talk about what she is feeling, and ask for assistance. Her internal dialogue and her ability to seek assistance significantly improve both her ability to effectively cope when she experiences distress and her ability to tap into her resiliency and rebound to her former level of functioning.

While going through the distressing aftermath of her accident, Michaela will most likely work to learn new skills to manage emotions and may experience them working effectively, which will strengthen her belief she is a competent individual. She will probably also experience people as effectively meeting her needs when she reaches out to them, which will strengthen her belief in others being dependable. These new experiences will cause her attachment style to become even more stable than it was prior to the accident.

Deliberately learning and practicing skills along with deliberately choosing to risk putting yourself in situations where others have the opportunity to meet your needs, extend love and acceptance to you, and remind you of your identity in Christ creates new, powerful experiential memories that begin to replace "bedrock" memories that taught something different—no matter what your attachment style!

Preoccupied Attachment Style

In contrast to individuals with secure attachments, individuals with preoccupied attachments do not view themselves as capable and competent. Their early experiential memories may have been ones in which they were given inappropriately difficult tasks that caused them to consistently experience failure, and their caregivers were not attuned enough to adjust what was being expected of them. Conversely, the tasks may have been developmentally appropriate but their caregivers were fearful the child would be unsuccessful or experience failure, overfunctioned for the child, or did not encourage the child to take risks and learn from unsuccessful attempts. These caregivers are often referred to as "helicopter parents." Their well-intentioned attempts to protect their child from negative experiences actually produce a negative self-concept within the child. Their constant attention to the child and unwillingness to allow the child to experience frustration and failure teach that the parent is an all-knowing, all-powerful, and dependable adult the child needs at all times to be okay. These children grow up to firmly believe others are dependable and competent to meet their needs while they, on the other hand, are incompetent and incapable of managing their own emotions or taking care of themselves.

Children who develop this internal belief system become preoccupied with having someone else in their world at all times and making sure this other individual is aware of them, taking care of them, and unwilling to leave or abandon them. They are extremely sensitive to where individuals they are attached to are at, what they are feeling, and what they perceive these individuals want them to be doing. As individuals with preoccupied attachments become adults, they have difficulty making their own decisions. They are often willing to be in unhealthy, even abusive, relationships just to have someone with them, someone who takes care of them, and someone who tells them what to do.

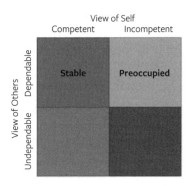

Individuals with preoccupied attachments form 13.62 percent of the general population[10] and, understandably, have fewer skills with which to handle anxiety. Their primary caregivers calmed them when they were upset and attended to their emotions but did not provide space for the child to practice soothing themselves or develop their own ability to regulate emotions. This leaves individuals with preoccupied attachments with an intense fear of abandonment or doing something to upset the person they feel dependent upon for their well-being. Just as with individuals with stable attachments, those with preoccupied attachments can have a variable sense of their own capability and the dependability of others.

Both the lack of emotion regulation skills and the fear of losing people they feel dependent upon can contribute to chronic worry and to anxiety disorders. For example, if Tommy has a preoccupied attachment style and is struggling with symptoms of acute stress disorder after having been in a near-fatal car accident, his internal self-talk is likely to be about the things he was unable to do when he was in the accident, his inability to handle his emotions currently, and his inability to make sure bad things won't happen in the future. He probably has difficulty being by himself without experiencing an increase in his distressing emotions and will tend to overvalue the help others give him while devaluing his own actions during and following the accident. His inability to self-soothe or view himself as someone who successfully navigated a horrific situation will increase his feelings of being out of control and overwhelmed—all of which will feed anxiety and worry. Like Michaela, Tommy can choose to use this as an opportunity to learn and practice new skills around managing his emotions. He can also surround himself with dependable people who are consistently present while encouraging him to do things for himself, celebrating his successes, and refusing to overfunction for him. If he does this, he will begin to view himself as more capable and be less preoccupied with needing others in order to be okay. This, in turn, will contribute to a greater ability to manage worry and anxiety in his life.

Avoidant Attachment Style

Up to this point, we have been examining attachment styles where the primary caregivers are dependable and adequately meet the needs of the child (55.24 percent of the general population).[11] What happens if the caregivers are not dependable and/or don't adequately meet the needs of the child? Imagine being an infant who wakes up alone, hungry, and wearing a wet diaper.

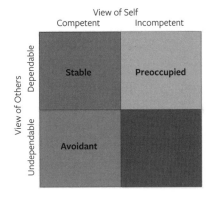

You begin to cry out in your distress, and one of three things happens:

- Your cries go unanswered no matter how long and how loud you cry.
- Someone arrives, but this individual feels incompetent and overwhelmed themselves and is unsure what to do to calm you. They become distressed and break down into tears, creating even more anxiety and distress for you.
- The individual who arrives is angry you are crying, yells at you to shut up, and roughly shoves a bottle into your mouth without ever touching you. They then stare at the tv in the other room while you eat.

In each of these situations, your caregiver is not attuned to what you need emotionally and physically and doesn't calmly meet those needs, which leaves you in distress.

Infants whose primary caregivers are unable or unavailable to meet their emotional and physical needs will continue to cry until the distress is simply too overwhelming for them. When the distress goes on for too long or becomes too overwhelming, they emotionally shut down and stop crying because they stop feeling.

They learn to take care of themselves by disconnecting from their own emotions and from everyone around them. Their experiential memories are of others being undependable and unavailable. They become self-reliant and find ways to feel better—often by becoming high achievers or by seeking ways of feeling pleasure no matter what the cost. While it would seem as though these individuals should experience low levels of anxiety because they see themselves as competent, their view of themselves is tumultuous since it is based upon performance and accomplishment. Their self-confidence is actually a façade distancing them from everyone. Infants raised in Romanian orphanages where they were deprived of the ability to form healthy attachments with caregivers had "double the 20 percent rate of anxiety symptoms found in children assigned to quality foster care settings."[12]

Deep wounds are created when our needs are not met and others don't speak words of identity into our lives. God created us to live interconnected lives. Individuals with avoidant attachments still have this need but have learned to avoid their awareness of the need by shutting down emotionally. They substitute externally pleasurable activities or accomplishments for relationships. This leaves them with an extremely limited ability to actually encounter and manage emotions. Additionally, they usually have limited skills to use in asking for and receiving the things they need. All of this combines to increase their susceptibility to anxiety and worry as well as equip them with fewer resources to tap into when they experience anxiety. For example, if Jane has an avoidant attachment style and experiences symptoms of acute stress disorder after being involved in a near-fatal car accident, she will have difficulty letting anyone know she is experiencing distress. Her own internal skills for managing emotion include either shutting down or medicating in some fashion. She may attempt to disconnect from her emotions by using an internal dialogue like, *You're fine. This isn't an issue, so just don't think about it.*

If she is able to disconnect from her emotions using this sort of self-talk, the events that created the acute stress disorder will remain unprocessed and will be as powerful six months after the event as they were the day of the event. She will need to either continue disconnecting emotionally every time she experiences these symptoms or face a flood of emotions she has a limited ability to manage. She will also have difficulty being connected to others who could empathetically support her in the midst of her distress, provide reassurance, and assist her as she works toward health. She may throw herself into work, fill her evenings with binge-watching tv, or self-medicate with alcohol or sedatives to help herself sleep. None of these activities will address her underlying anxiety and, eventually, her unhealthy coping skills will begin to cause additional problems she will need to address.

For Jane to move toward health, she will need assistance in learning ways of managing her emotions rather than shutting them down and avoiding them. She will also need experiences of being vulnerable in relationships and having her needs for connection, love, and support validated and appropriately responded to. Given that her experiences in the past have told her people are not reliable, this will feel incredibly risky for Jane. She will need to avoid the trap of simply waiting for people to disappoint her, because, inevitably, someone will make a mistake along the way and this will give her permission to continue believing others are not trustworthy instead of developing healthier beliefs.

Fearful Attachment Style

Individuals with stable, preoccupied, or avoidant attachment styles all experienced a consistent pattern within their life. The caregivers in their world were consistently either dependable or undependable, allowing them to consistently see themselves as competent or incompetent. Individuals with fearful attachments have a very different experience. In their world, nothing was consistent. Sometimes their primary caregivers were available and met their needs well. Other times, these same caregivers were either unavailable or punitive. Sometimes they were encouraged to try new things and praised for attempts whether or not they were successful.

Other times they were treated as incompetent or punished for not knowing how to do something without needing to practice and learn. These experiences created chaotic internal and external environments for the child, leaving them unsure of what could be depended upon and what they were capable of.

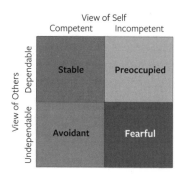

Individuals with a fearful attachment comprise 26.14 percent of the general population and often come from environments where there is either extreme dysfunction or abuse.[13] Having been unable to answer the questions of whether or not they are competent and whether or not others are dependable, they live in constant fear of mis-assessing either their capability or others' dependability. They tend to be rather black-and-white in their thinking and swing between extremes. In one situation, they are sure they are totally competent and others don't know what they are talking about and are undependable. In the next situation, they view themselves as totally incompetent and dependent upon others whom they both cling to and demand from. When they form relationships, the people they are in relationship with often describe feeling like they are repeatedly drawn in close and then abruptly pushed away for no apparent reason. Within relationships, individuals with fearful attachments often have intense emotional reactions to small experiences of undependability, like their partner being fifteen minutes late getting home from work, while simultaneously demanding extravagant expressions as proof of love and devotion.

Individuals with fearful attachments live their lives feeling anxious about every decision they make and are unable to feel comfortable or relax in relationships. While this does not necessarily mean they will develop an anxiety disorder, it certainly heightens this possibility and gives them fewer coping skills should one develop. For example, if Vincent has a fearful attachment style and is struggling with acute stress disorder after being in a near-fatal car accident, he will be overwhelmed by his emotions and will have only limited ability to consistently utilize skills to manage his emotions and calm himself. Some days he will manage well, and other days he will feel helpless to manage his feelings and demand others do it for him. Simultaneously, he will both demand others care for him and rebuff their efforts to help him. Without the skills to consistently regulate his own emotions and have relationships where others are allowed to consistently care for him in healthy ways, he will remain stuck in crisis. External attempts made by others to move him out of this will be futile.

Vincent will have the most difficulty moving toward health because neither his sense of himself nor his view of others is consistent and trustworthy. For him to move toward health, he would need to begin strengthening his self-soothing and emotion regulation skills so he can consistently utilize them without being overwhelmed. He would also need to risk allowing others to be present with him without either demanding they care for him in unhealthy ways or pushing them away and refusing their attempts to provide appropriate care. This process would take time and consistent work from both him and the others involved in his life, but would result in experiencing much less chaos and anxiety.

Your Attachment Style

I suspect many of you identified with at least some of the descriptions contained in this chapter. No one, other than Jesus, has a perfectly stable attachment style. This means we have all had times when we did not experience ourselves as competent or others as dependable to meet our needs. As a result, we developed coping strategies—some of which were unhealthy and left us with characteristics of a preoccupied, avoidant, or fearful attachment. To help you identify both your primary attachment style and where you might have developed unhealthy coping skills from other attachment styles, circle the number of each statement below that fits you:

1. I often worry the people I am closest to will stop loving me.
2. I fear once someone gets to know the real me, they won't like who I am.
3. When I don't have deep, emotionally connected relationships in my life, I feel anxious and incomplete.
4. When someone I am very close to is distant or unavailable, I find myself fearful they may find someone else whom they would rather be close to.
5. When I express emotion or feelings to the people I am closest to, I am fearful they will not feel the same about me.
6. I think about the people I am close to a lot.
7. I tend to very quickly become close and emotionally connected to people.

8. I am very sensitive to the moods of the people I am close to.

9. I worry that if the people I am close to leave, I will have difficulty finding others to be close to.

10. If someone I've been close to begins to act cold and distant, I worry I've done something wrong.

11. I tend to avoid telling someone I am close to I am upset because I don't want to damage the relationship.

12. I find it easy to be affectionate with people I am close to.

13. I feel comfortable depending on people I am close to.

14. I am generally satisfied with my close relationships.

15. I have little difficulty expressing my needs and wants to people I am close to.

16. I can easily be emotionally present with people and empathically connect to where they are at emotionally when they are upset.

17. I am not easily threatened by the strengths of the people around me.

18. I believe most people are essentially honest and dependable.

19. I am comfortable sharing my personal thoughts and feelings with the people I am close to.

20. An argument with people I am close to doesn't usually cause me to question our relationship.

21. Sometimes people see me as boring because I don't create much drama in relationships.

22. When I disagree with someone, I feel comfortable expressing my opinions.

23. If someone I'm close to begins to act cold and distant, I may wonder what's happening, but I am relatively sure it is probably not about me or they will tell me if it is.

24. I find I bounce back quickly after someone leaves my life. I can easily put someone who has left my life out of my mind.

25. I find it difficult to be emotionally present with people and to match their emotions when they are feeling upset.

26. My independence is a very high value.

27. I prefer not to share my innermost feelings with the people I am close to.

28. I find it difficult to depend on people.

29. I sometimes feel angry or annoyed with people I am close to when we are having deep conversations containing intense emotions.

30. It makes me nervous when people get too close to me emotionally.

31. During conflict, I can get to the place where I express emotions in ways that cause others to distance themselves from me either emotionally or physically.

32. The people I am close to often want me to be more emotionally vulnerable than I am comfortable with.

33. When someone likes me, I find myself initially interested but rapidly lose interest in the relationship.

34. I don't like feeling people are dependent on me.

35. If someone I've been close to begins to act cold and distant, I find myself feeling indifferent about it.[14]

Total number of circles 1–11:	_____	Preoccupied Attachment
Total number of circles 12–23:	_____	Stable Attachment
Total number of circles 24–35:	_____	Avoidant Attachment

Take note of the category where you had the most circles as this is most likely your primary attachment style. If you find your numbers evenly spread between preoccupied and avoidant, this would suggest you might have a fearful attachment style.

This inventory is not conclusive. It is simply a guide to help you identify what might be true in your life. Attachment styles are neither right nor wrong. Understanding our primary attachment style can help us grow and learn ways to manage our emotions and our relationships better. This, in turn, can decrease our worry and anxiety.

While I referenced healing coming through learning skills and having healthy experiences with others, ultimately it is our experience of God's love and our experience of him speaking identity over us that provides healing. However, we experience wounding in relationships with human beings and God pours his love and his words of identity through human beings to bring healing to those wounds. We will talk about how our wounds affect our image of God and ways we can experience God's healing love and affirmation later in this book.

CHAPTER FIVE

SOCIAL ENVIRONMENTS AFFECT ANXIETY

A s a child, every afternoon I climbed aboard a school bus for the bouncy, winding journey to my house. As the trip wore on and my stop neared, I inevitably felt my body tense in anticipation. My biggest fear was arriving home to find my parents had moved while I was gone. This fear was so strong that, on the one occasion I did actually arrive home to find an empty house, I panicked and ran frantically to stop the bus before it had a chance to complete its turnaround in my driveway. Amid sobs, I announced to the bus driver that I had been abandoned. The kindly bus driver beckoned his frantic charge back onto the bus, drove me to a neighbor's house, and explained the situation to the woman who answered the door. The neighbor (who I don't think knew me) took charge of me and watched for my mother's car to make its way down the dusty gravel road. When the family station wagon passed—about five minutes later—the neighbor returned me to a very frustrated mother. She had been detained at an appointment and was a few minutes behind the bus with no way to warn me.

To my mother, my fear made absolutely no sense. She had never abandoned me and knew I was both old enough and capable enough to manage the few minutes I would be alone prior to her return. I, however, did not see the world through the same lens. At this stage in my life, we had moved at least one time per school year with what seemed to me to be no warning and no reason. Each time, the move would be announced and within a few months we had changed homes and changed schools—often with no opportunity to say goodbye to those left behind. For a young, firstborn child whose brain liked routine, predictability, and having a sense of control over her environment, these moves created an underlying, palpable uncertainty around the permanence of anything in my life. My social environment growing up contributed to an ongoing, low-level worry about who would leave me and whether I could be okay if they did.

While I can now look at this incident and see the humor in it, my social environment growing up continues to impact which situations create anxiety for me. I am aware of this factor and can manage it but still find changing environments and the possibility of people leaving my life anxiety-provoking.

The environment we live in currently and environments we have lived in throughout the course of our life contribute to the level of anxiety we live with on a consistent basis. These environments also impact whether we will develop an anxiety disorder. Just like genetics or psychological factors alone cannot be proven to cause an anxiety disorder, neither can the stress of our social environment. However, considerable research has been conducted around the hypothesis that the more your genetics are predisposed toward developing an anxiety disorder, the less stress there needs to be in your environment for an anxiety disorder to develop.[1] In the last chapter, we looked at how our experiences—particularly those with our primary caregivers—influence what we grow to believe about ourselves and the world around us. In this chapter, we will expand upon this to look at how the environment we live in, combined with our temperament, can influence the level of anxiety we experience.

Sources of Stress

All of us experience stress in various forms over the course of our life. The more stress present in our life, the unhealthier this stress is, and the fewer resources we have to deal with the stressors, the more likely we are to experience ongoing worry or an anxiety disorder as a result. Stress is easy to see when we think in terms of large, negative experiences like being in a war zone, being the victim of abuse, surviving a natural disaster, or being involved in a major accident. While these are certainly traumatic and stressful events profoundly influencing those involved, stress encompasses many different types of experiences—both positive and negative. The term *stress*, as it is currently used, was coined in 1936 by Hans Selye, who defined it as "the non-specific response of the body to any demand for change."[2] While many different mechanisms exist to categorize stressors, I have found it helpful to think of stress as coming from five different types of experiences: unmet needs, receiving what is unneeded, onetime events, betrayal, and sustained distress.

Unmet Needs

Every individual is designed by God with needs. Psychologist Abraham Maslow formed these into a "hierarchy of needs," which can generally be described as:

1. **Basic Care.** Having your needs for food, water, shelter, warmth, and sleep met.

2. **Safety.** Consistently experiencing your environment as being one that protects you and feels secure.

3. **Connection, Love, and Belonging.** Experiencing yourself as connected in a healthy way to individuals in your life at home, work, and/or school whom you trust to unconditionally love you, show you affection, and receive those same things from you as you extend them.

4. **Personal Worth and Value.** Receiving consistent messages from others which cause you to believe you are a unique, worthwhile, precious individual made in the image of God. Knowing you can accomplish things, master tasks, and function independently in ways that are respected by others.

5. **Intellectual.** Receiving safe opportunities and encouragement to explore, learn, and understand yourself and the world around you in ways that create meaning and make your environment predictable. This exploration should include affirmation and growth of gifts and talents.

6. **Artistic/Creative.** Having opportunities to develop and express appreciation for beauty and creativity.

7. **Fulfillment.** Having the opportunities and resources to successfully pursue personal, professional, and relational desires.

8. **Spiritual.** Having a pathway to fellowship with God that leads you to see beyond yourself and be motivated to live a life centered around this relationship rather than self-gratification.[3]

When these needs are unmet, they create stress. They can be unmet because parents, spouses, or others in your life refuse to provide for them. At other times, they can feel unmet even when people who love you are valiantly attempting to meet your needs. Examples of stress produced through unmet needs include things like: a parent who spends money needed for food on drugs, a teacher who ridicules students in class for answering questions wrong, a boss who consistently looks past you and your work without validating your presence or the work you do, a bully harassing you online or in person, or a church that teaches artistic pursuits are evil and "good Christians" couldn't possibly be involved in the art world. While each of these seem like overt acts that create stress, the same sort of stress is also created when, for example, a young couple lives each month unsure they will be able to pay the rent, have money for groceries, and keep the electricity turned on with the income from their minimum wage jobs. Sometimes needs may be experienced as unmet even when it appears they are being met; the experience I shared at the beginning of this chapter would be such an example. My parents felt they were providing a safe and secure environment for me. It also undoubtedly looked that way to everyone observing externally. However, I experienced my environment as neither secure nor dependable, and thus it was traumatizing and anxiety provoking. Needless to say, no one has all their needs met at all times, so everyone experiences some stress connected to unmet needs.

Receiving What Is Unneeded

Each of the things listed on Maslow's hierarchy of needs is necessary for us to become and remain healthy. At the same time, there are many things we do not need—and receiving these can also create stress. American culture is currently filled with the subtle (and sometimes not so subtle) message *If I could only get to XX then I could be happy*. Buying into and believing this message has caused us to fill our lives with unneeded experiences, things, and people. This, in turn, creates stress and contributes to both worry and anxiety.

The belief that something we don't yet have will create happiness starts young! Think about it . . . what would happen if you gave a child everything they asked for, demanded, or thought they needed? My children wanted candy, no naps, no homework, no rules, no chores, no bedtime, every toy they passed in the store that caught their eye, to participate in multiple activities at school, to excel and be the best at all they tried, and to be friends with all the popular people. What would have happened if I had been able to and chosen to give them all those things? Whether or not you are a parent, you know chaos would have ensued and the likelihood of my children growing up to be well-adjusted, healthy adults would have gone down significantly. My example seems absurd . . . or does it? We live in a culture where children's lives are being scheduled from the time they wake up until the time they go to bed. They are involved in activities starting as young as two years old to ensure they are positioned for the "best opportunities." The result . . . an increase in stress-related illnesses, including anxiety disorders, and a decrease in children's actual performance.

The same is true in the adult world. The more we buy into the cultural belief that happiness and contentment will be achieved at some moment in the future when our expectations are met and our external goals are finally achieved, the more stress we create for ourselves and the less we truly appreciate the moment we are currently in.

According to the International Labour Organization (ILO), "Americans work 137 more hours per year than Japanese workers, 260 more hours per year than British workers, and 499 more hours per year than French workers."[4] Partially to facilitate this and partially as a result of this, in 2018 American adults spent more than eleven hours per day interacting with digital media.[5] This increase is due to the amount of time spent at work, checking email, scrolling through social media, and texting—all of which increase stress levels. Research has shown spending more time on smartphones results in an increase in symptoms of anxiety, depression, and stress.[6]

As we have increased the hours we work, possessions we have, and time we spend on digital media, our culture has also experienced an increase in anxiety disorders, suicide, and depression. As we push our children to do more, achieve more, and have more, they report higher levels of anxiety and stress. These are just two examples of how having unneeded things can contribute to higher levels of both worry and anxiety.

Onetime Events

If you were over the age of five in 2001, you can probably describe where you were when you heard about 9/11. Similarly, if you have been the bride or groom in a wedding, it is likely you can give a detailed account of the experience. Both are examples of onetime events that create a high level of stress in our lives. Stress is not connected to just the negative events in our life. Positive events also create stress, and the body reacts similarly to both positive and negative stress. I know a woman who needed hospitalization to treat a severe anxiety disorder after she got engaged. She had been looking forward to meeting a godly man and getting married, so she found it extremely difficult to comprehend why her body reacted to her engagement with panic and anxiety she could not control.

Onetime events like 9/11, being in a car accident, speaking in front of a large crowd, being assaulted, graduating from college, getting married, and leaving home (to name a few) can produce an intense physiological experience of fear, anxiety, and loss of control. An automobile accident that totals the car while everyone walks away unhurt, however, will most likely produce different short-term and long-term reactions for those involved than an automobile accident where you or someone you love is seriously injured or killed. The drivers in both may have a difficult time getting into a vehicle for the first time after the accident, but the more traumatic the event, the more likely the individual is to develop an anxiety disorder requiring treatment.

In addition to the severity of the event, the kind and amount of support the individual receives in the wake of the event also affects the level of anxiety they will experience. If you go through something traumatic and have a community of individuals who meet you where you are at emotionally, validate your experience, and support you as you move through the experience, you will return to your normal level of functioning faster than if you are left alone, your feelings or experiences are invalidated, or you are required to pretend nothing bad has happened.

Betrayal

We are born as individuals with a deep need to trust. All infants are dependent and need to trust the adults in their life to meet their needs. When we can trust the people and circumstances around us, it assuages our anxiety and allows us to focus on enjoying the individuals and experiences around us. Betrayal—whether actual or perceived—shatters our ability to trust whoever or whatever has betrayed us. Betrayal also makes it difficult to trust others who are close to you or enter your life after the betrayal. Betrayal occurs when we feel harmed by either the intentional or unintentional actions or omissions of someone we trust.[7] It happens whenever there is a "breaking or violation of a presumptive contract, trust, or confidence that produces moral and psychological conflict within a relationship amongst individuals, between organizations, or between individuals and organizations."[8]

Finding out your friend has taken what you shared in confidence and used it as part of another conversation, having a business partner take your idea and claim it as their own, finding out your spouse is sleeping with another individual, or finding out your parents lied to you by not telling you about your adoption as an infant are all forms of betrayal. In each case, what you believed to be trustworthy turned out not to be. When this happens, it shakes our ability to know what is and is not trustworthy and creates an underlying distrust of others. This, in turn, produces anxiety, loneliness, and resentment. Since it is impossible to know with absolute certainty we can trust others, we must develop the capacity to discern who should be trusted and to believe we can successfully navigate the pain involved if our trust is betrayed. If we are unable to find ways to do this, we will be relegated to a life filled with mistrust. Living governed by mistrust isolates us from the very things we need to feel safe, secure, and less anxious.

Sustained Distress

Individuals who are being physically, sexually, or emotionally abused live in sustained distress. Similarly, individuals who live in poverty or environments filled with violence are in a state of chronic, sustained distress. These situations seem obviously stressful to us and are routinely identified as such. What may not be as easy to identify is how sustained distress can also occur when your personality and your environment are at odds.

Friends of mine have two children born eighteen months apart. Their lives, from conception to delivery, looked very similar, and yet they came into this world with two very different personalities. From birth, their first daughter was quite content to be alone, and when she became upset, she found it relatively easy to calm herself. This young lady excelled when given a concrete set of tasks, rules, or goals. She was easily distressed by too many unexpected changes or too many people creating noise in her environment. Their second daughter, on the other hand, entered the world as an emotionally sensitive individual with a high need for the presence of others in her life. In contrast to her sister, this young lady could easily roll with the punches when things did not go as expected, rarely planned for her day, and found the chaos created by groups of people to be invigorating. As is often the case with individuals who are emotionally sensitive, she tended to personalize the behavior of others and struggled to calm herself when she became upset. Two children with the same parents, living in the same environment, and yet what was distressing to one invigorated the other—how can this be?

Our personality is both something wired into our genetic makeup and something formed as we grow and develop. Personality assessment tools like the Myers-Briggs or the Enneagram have given names to broad categories of personality characteristics and can help individuals know what things will be helpful or unhelpful given these personality traits. For example, if you are an introvert—someone who is replenished and restored by alone time and would prefer spending time one-on-one with individuals—having a job requiring you to frequently engage in high levels of large-group interactions is bound to be chronically distressing. Likewise, if you are an extrovert—someone who thrives on social interaction—and your job is one where you work from home without human interaction for days at a time, you will experience an increased level of chronic stress. Similarly, if you are someone who requires a high level of structure and find it easiest to relax when everything around you is in order, you are going to find it difficult to maintain your emotional health if you are required to live or work in a chaotic and unstructured environment.

While it might seem these personality traits are easily identified and adjusted to, in reality we often expect ourselves to be different from who we really are. We also tend to expect the people around us to know what we need and adapt to these needs by changing who they are. I frequently see individuals in my practice who are highly distressed because they have been attempting to turn themselves into who they think they "ought" to be so they can be successful, please their spouse, or raise the perfect children rather than embracing the way they were constructed by God and learning how to effectively function using the strengths these characteristics give them. Until we understand our basic temperament and learn how to create environments for ourselves where we can function effectively, we are destined to experience ongoing stress, worry, and anxiety.

Mitigating Social and Environmental Stressors

If you are like me, you read through the chapter with a rising sense of *But I can't change this or this or this . . . so now what?* While there are many factors in our environment we cannot change, there are still things we can do to lessen their impact upon our stress level and the anxiety they produce in our lives. Below are some action steps you can take to help reduce the stress and anxiety you may experience in each of the five areas we discussed.

Unmet Needs

Read through the list below to help identify ways you can continue doing things that meet your basic needs and work to improve in areas where your needs may be unmet.

1. Basic Care

   Are you eating well-balanced and nutritious meals every day? If not, what is one measurable thing you could do to work toward this goal?

   Are you getting eight hours of sleep per night? If not, how could you get at least fifteen minutes more of sleep each night?

   Do you drink at least sixty-four ounces of water each day? If not, what is one thing you can do to increase your water intake?

2. Safety

What is one thing you can do each day to help create a safe place where you can relax for at least thirty minutes?

3. Connection, Love, and Belonging

Who have you connected with today, and how have they shown you they care about you? Take a moment to reflect upon how it feels to know this individual cares about you.

Who have you worked to show love and affection to today? How would you like to be more deliberate about this in the future?

4. Personal Worth and Value

Think back on your day and make a list of at least three things you did that you feel good about, others thanked you for, or others said you did well.

Take a moment to celebrate these accomplishments and thank God for giving you the ability to do these things.

5. Intellectual

What is one thing you have learned in the last week?

What is one thing you would like to grow in your ability to understand or do? What can you do to begin this process?

6. Artistic/Creative

What is one thing that brings beauty or creativity into your life? Consider things like sitting outside and enjoying nature, listening to good music, or coloring. Make plans to do something that brings beauty or creativity into your life in the next week.

7. Fulfillment

What is one personal or professional goal you have? As you think about this goal, is it something you want because you think it will make you happy or something you want because it will push you to be everything God created you to be? If it is something you think you need in order to be happy, consider what it would take to feel fulfilled and happy right now. If it is something that would push you to become everything God created you to be, what is one step you could take to move in this direction?

8. Spiritual

How do you connect with God and enjoy fellowship with him? If this is a foreign idea, what is one thing you could do to build an understanding of having an ongoing intimate connection with your Father? If you were able to identify things that allow you to feel intimately connected, how will you work to make room for these things in your life routinely? As you connect with God, what is one thing you would like to do with him to help advance his kingdom here on earth?

Receiving What Is Unneeded

1. Do you tend to be someone who believes you will be happy someday when you accomplish XX? If so, what would it take for you to be content with the things you have right now?

2. What things do you identify as being present in your life that are unnecessary and may be causing you to experience increased anxiety and stress? What is one step you could take to begin eliminating these things or changing how you think about them?

3. Work to set limits around when your work day begins and ends. This is especially important in terms of email. Consider setting limits around the last time you will check your email and send replies during your day, then let everything

else wait until morning. Also, consider waiting until you get to work to check your email in the morning instead of doing it when you first wake up or over breakfast.

4. What are three ground rules that would allow you to limit the negative impact of too much technology? You might consider no phones at the dinner table, no phones in the bedroom, or even setting your phone to airplane mode while you are meeting with your friends, putting the kids to bed, or going on a date with your spouse.

5. Consider taking a digital sabbatical. Find an hour, a day, a week, or even longer when you switch off everything digital and disengage from all social media.

Onetime Events

As you read through this section, what are the onetime events in your life that continue to affect you? If we use my example from the beginning of the chapter, I am aware a fear of abandonment continues to influence my life. By being aware of it, I can identify when it is influencing my thoughts, feelings, and behaviors. I can also choose to make conscious decisions about how I want to counter this. As you think about the onetime events you have identified, how are they affecting you currently? What is one thing you could do to minimize this? If you find the events you have identified are having a considerable negative impact or you don't know how to lessen their impact, you may want to consider talking to someone who could help you with this.

Betrayal

How have you experienced betrayal in your life? What did you learn from this? Are there ways you continue to function out of distrust that create anxiety or fear as a regular part of your life?

If so, what is one step you could take to move away from mistrust and toward healthy trust? If you struggle to answer this question, it may be important to talk with someone about how to resolve this in your life.

Sustained Distress

What are one or two important things you know about your personality? If you have trouble answering this, consider taking a personality inventory to help you identify your personality traits. Once you identify important parts of your personality, look for places in your life where your personality and the environment around you are not well aligned. Consider whether this misalignment is occurring because you are attempting to make yourself into something other than who God created you to be. If this is the case, what is one step you could take toward accepting yourself the way God made you? Next, what is one thing you could do to begin aligning your environment with your personality? For example, if you are an introvert working in a highly social career, you may want to consider setting aside your lunch hour each day to be alone and recenter so you are ready for the afternoon. If you are an extrovert married to an introvert, expecting your partner to be as social as you are will never work. You and your spouse may want to discuss how you can get your need for connection met while respecting your partner's need for alone time.

While we cannot mitigate all the stress and anxiety created by our social environment, we can work to take good care of ourselves, make sure our needs are met in healthy ways, and create spaces where our environment and our personality align as ways of limiting the impact our social environment has upon our level of anxiety.

CHAPTER SIX

OUR VIEW OF GOD AFFECTS ANXIETY

G od loves me, but he doesn't really like me very much," was how I answered someone walking with me as I struggled to make sense of some events in my life. This answer to a seemingly innocent question revealed a deep belief about God driving much of my emotional distress and constant need for perfection. I believed I had to be "good enough" to earn God's approval. No matter how hard I tried and how many things I got right, there was always this voice in my head announcing the things I hadn't gotten right. I concluded at an early age that this was the voice of God letting me know I still hadn't met his expectations.

I wish my experience was an anomaly and most people have a healthy, accurate understanding of who God is and how he feels about them. Unfortunately, this is not the case. No one, not even theologians who spend their lives studying God, has a perfect understanding of God. We are finite beings, which makes our understanding of any subject limited. God is infinite and we can never fully understand him. However, this doesn't mean we have to live with flawed understandings and experiences of God—like mine—that create and feed anxiety.

As I discussed in chapter 4, there is a difference between factual memory (2 + 2 = 4) and experiential memory (parents applauding as we hit the T-ball). Our experiences create a framework through which we understand ourselves and the world around us. In this chapter, we will look at how our experiences influence our understanding of God and his interactions with us.

I want to start with a reminder that our experiential understanding can often be different than our factual understanding. When I announced God loved me but didn't like me, it exposed a deep divide between what I factually knew to be true of God and the experiences that formed my beliefs about God. I knew God loved me. I had memorized and could quote Scriptures saying this was true. However, my experiences were not formed based upon these Scriptures. The facts created the first part of my statement— God loves me—while my experiences created the second part—he doesn't like me.

Our understanding of who God is and how he feels about us is often formed before we are old enough to use words as our primary form of communication and before we can reason abstractly. Children under the age of five store memories primarily in the form of pictures and visceral sensations filled with emotions. For example, my first conscious memory is of sitting in the back of my parents' car, watching my mother cry in the front seat as she held my brother and my father angrily drive the car at very high speeds. It is a visceral experience without thoughts connected to it. The memory has no context of its own and is simply an experience of seeing the most powerful people in my life upset, angry, and behaving in ways that made me fearful the car might crash while I sat helpless, alone, and afraid.

When I was an adolescent, this memory gained context when my parents recounted the story of my eighteen-month-old brother drinking out of a pop bottle my father had filled with gasoline for the lawnmower and then set down on the sidewalk while he finished his repairs. Hearing the story made sense of my memory intellectually. However, the experience and the conclusions I drew as a result occurred long before the context was added and were not necessarily changed just because I now had context.

The ability to reason in the abstract is a capacity that doesn't solidify until adolescence. This means, prior to adolescence, unless children can see it, hear it, touch it, or taste it, they don't really understand it. In my elementary math teaching methods class, I spent hours learning how to make abstract concepts into concrete experiences. We would take blocks and have students count them so the number 2 (an abstract concept) was connected to a concrete experience of touching two blocks. Having this experience meant when they saw the number 2 on a worksheet they would connect it to the picture memory of physically touching the two blocks.

God is an abstract concept in that we can't see, hear, touch, or taste him in concrete, tangible ways. As children, to form an understanding of who God is, we look for concrete experiences to hook to the abstract concept of "God." Sunday school, church, and our parents teach us God is powerful and strong. This causes us to hook our understanding of God to the strongest and most powerful people in our life and simply assume God is a bigger version of these people. All of this is done without conscious thought and creates a preliminary view of who God is and how he feels about us by the time we are five to seven years old.

By the time we learn to read (also about ages five to seven), we already have a framework for who God is and how he feels about us. We read Scripture through the lens created by this framework and selectively attend to verses supporting our understanding of who God is. I still own the first Bible I wrote in. Even a casual perusal reveals a plethora of underlined verses about what good Christians should and shouldn't do. The verses referencing his kindness, graciousness, understanding, and care are untouched. I read Scripture through the lens of needing to earn God's approval, and this determined which verses I was drawn to.

Each of us has distinct experiences that formed our understanding—both accurate and inaccurate—of who God is and how he feels about us. Notice I said *experiences*, not reality. It is important to remember experience doesn't equal reality. Experience represents just that—what you experienced. As the parent of two grown children, I am consistently amazed at their recollected experiences of childhood compared to what I was attempting to provide for them and my memories of their childhood.

It is important to own your experiences in a validating, safe environment and then work through the thoughts, feelings, and behaviors connected to these experiences. It is equally important not to declare your experiences to be the ultimate truth about what happened or to blame others for "doing this to me."

Our concept of God is originally formed based upon information that cannot represent God completely and accurately, because it is formed based upon our young brain's interpretation of experiences with fallible human beings. Our brains are also constantly taking in new information, calling up similar experiences from our past, integrating this new information with the old information, and refiling the newly transformed information. This process, referred to by psychologists as reconsolidation,[1] means our image of God is also changed by the things we encounter over time. Thus, even if our original experiences of powerful authority figures are loving and kind, if we later have a series of experiences where powerful authority figures feel demanding, uncaring, or uninterested, this will be added to our original experiences and will alter our image of God. Our brains have remarkable plasticity, which means that throughout our lifetime our understanding of who God is and who we are will be continually growing and changing.

Much of the process described above happens unconsciously as we experience life. However, we can also deliberately engage in activities that cause our original experiences to be changed. Consciously engaging in activities that help us to develop and maintain a healthy factual and experiential understanding of God requires us to understand how our current concept of God is distorted. While there are many ways of talking about distorted images of God, we will talk about six common distortions of God in this chapter. The examples used to shed light on each of these images will be of ones formed during childhood, but it is important to remember experiences throughout our life can contribute to forming each of them.

Unpleasable Boss God

Individuals who struggle with the distortion of "Unpleasable Boss God" find themselves caught in the trap of attempting to do all the "dos" found in Scripture while simultaneously attempting to avoid all of the "don'ts." The inability to consistently do all the right things leaves you feeling condemned, ashamed, and unacceptable. No matter how much you do right, there is always at least one nagging thing you "could" have or "should" have done, and, because you didn't, you have fallen short once more. God's expectations of you are always just beyond reach, leaving you constantly striving and fearful of falling short once again.

The paradigm of the "Unpleasable Boss God" forms when a child's experience of the most important people in their life is one in which these individuals spend most of their time correcting the child or telling the child what was done wrong and needs to be done differently next time.

If you are someone who struggles with "Unpleasable Boss God," this doesn't mean the important adults in your life were necessarily unpleasable. It does mean your childhood experiences left you feeling unable to please the people whose opinion mattered most to you. The desire to please both God and people drives your life. You anxiously consider what they might want, what they might feel, and how you might disappoint them if you can't perfectly meet their expectations. This drive leaves you constantly on alert and attempting to read the minds of those you care about so you don't disappoint them.

I'm Outta Here God

Some individuals live with the constant niggling fear they are going to do something that causes God to leave them. Scripture verses that even hint you might be able to lose your salvation and be thrown into the lake of fire feed this fear. In an attempt to be sure God never leaves, you constantly try to do and say the right things while simultaneously feeling insecure about whether God truly sees you as his child whom he loves and will never leave nor forsake. This fear of abandonment may also cause you to remain distant from God to steel yourself emotionally for when he inevitably abandons you.

Individuals struggling with the "I'm Outta Here God" frequently experienced what felt like or literally was abandonment in their life. When this occurred, the concluded it happened as a result of something they did or said. The abandonment may have been someone important dying or someone leaving because of divorce. Children who are ill and spend extended periods of time in the hospital can experience abandonment even when their parents are attempting to provide appropriate care. Conversely, sometimes children experience abandonment when an adult in their world experiences a prolonged illness and is away from them. When children perceive abandonment, it is common for them to conclude they have done something wrong or were unacceptable, and this caused the person they valued to leave. For example, divorce is never a child's fault, but most children worry the parent who left did so because they were too difficult, made too many mistakes, said mean things, or didn't love the parent well enough. Even after being told repeatedly this is not the case, they may still fear it is true. If you are someone who struggles with "I'm Outta Here God," you may find yourself living on pins and needles, attempting to do the right things to keep God present while simultaneously living with an impending sense of doom caused by the belief he will eventually leave.

Just Get Over It God

Individuals who experience "Just Get Over It God" feel he is emotionally unavailable and are convinced he is only concerned with the cold, hard facts of life and their ability to "get the job done." You see God as unsympathetic and uncaring. As others talk about a close relationship with God, you ask yourself, *Why would God care about my problems?* or *Why would God want to hear how I feel?* You see God as concerned about what you do, but not about what you feel. Beyond that, you may even believe God doesn't want you to feel and is displeased or angry if you are struggling with painful feelings.

The "Just Get Over It God" paradigm develops when children grow up experiencing their feelings as discounted, minimized, or wrong/bad. This is particularly prevalent among American men, who are taught "Big boys don't cry" or "Don't be a sissy." While society invalidates men's emotions, this is not the only way invalidation can occur. Many children experience emotional invalidation as a regular part of their life, even though the adults in their world are unaware this is the child's experience. Authority figures say things like, "It's just your feelings that got hurt," or "There's nothing to be afraid of here" to move children out of their emotions. When caregivers do this, they are inadvertently communicating to the child that their emotions are not valid, important, or even normal. If you grew up feeling your emotions didn't matter or were shamed for having emotions, you may find yourself fearing God's response to your emotions. Individuals struggling in this way often attempt to stuff or minimize all feelings except the "positive" emotions. However, fear, pain, and hurt refuse to be discounted and will show up as things like perfectionism, risk avoidance, depression, anxiety, and other medical conditions.

Do Not Disturb God

Similar to individuals who struggle with "Just Get Over It God," individuals experience "Do Not Disturb God" as uninterested. While "Just Get Over It God" is uninterested in feelings, "Do Not Disturb God" simply doesn't have time for the daily activities and struggles of your life. He is present in the distance, much like the President of the United States, but doesn't really know or care what is going on in your daily life. He makes the rules, tells you what you should do, and expects you to get it done. How you get it done and how it impacts you are of little concern to him. All that matters is accomplishing the task in the right timeframe and without breaking any of his commands in the process. If you struggle with "Do Not Disturb God," you often feel the tasks you have been given are as overwhelming as climbing Mt. Everest without the benefit of a guide. You go through life feeling ill-equipped, incompetent, and alone with no one to help you figure it out.

Individuals who struggle with "Do Not Disturb God" often grew up in environments where the adults in their world were constantly busy and worried about their jobs, their relationships, and their finances. Children often perceive these adults as always working, tired, overwhelmed, and anxious about their own worlds with no time for the child. Children in this environment often conclude they need to figure it out on their own because the adults don't have time to help or would be inconvenienced by being asked to stop and help. Often adults who communicate messages like this to children grew up in an environment where children were "seen and not heard," so they have limited skill in attending to a child's needs. They tune in temporarily when the child has a sporting event, recital, or new report card, but then check back out and leave the child alone to navigate life and manage their inner world.

Maybe I Will and Maybe I Won't God

Individuals who experience "Maybe I Will and Maybe I Won't God" are never sure whether they can trust God to show up. While you are sure he has made promises, you don't trust he will keep his promises. You are never sure how to determine which promises he will keep and when he will make some sort of excuse and back out. It feels as though some days he loves you, is in your corner, and is following through on everything he promises. Other days he is willing to toss you aside in anger because he believes you have wronged him in some fashion. Your reaction to this unpredictable sense of God's faithfulness is to go it on your own and believe if you can just "get it right," everything will be okay. You attempt to pull yourself up by your bootstraps and get yourself through whatever muck each day may give you. You live by the motto "Everyone for themselves," even in your relationship with God.

This "Maybe I Will and Maybe I Won't God" mindset develops when a child perceives the adults in their world as just that—unpredictable. One day the adult you care about seems cheerful, attentive, and enthralled with your world. The next day this same adult seems angry, inattentive, and oblivious to your experience of the situation. These adults sometimes become enraged over what seems to be a small mistake, while at other times they are forgiving and overlook a much bigger mistake. When the adult is upset or fails to keep a promise, you may be told you are to blame. You initially believe if you try harder, the adult will become reliable. However, eventually you give up on this and conclude you can't trust people (or God).

Now You're Going to Get It God

If you struggle with an image of God as "Now You're Going to Get It God," you experience him as easily angered, demanding, hurtful, and cruel. You constantly live on pins and needles, believing if you don't think the right way, feel the right things, and act in just the right way, God is going to punish you and punish you severely. Old Testament stories where the ground opens up and swallows hundreds of people for their sin support your conviction that God is watching for you to mess up so he can punish you. "Now You're Going to Get It God" is unapproachable and scary, and his underlying intention toward you is to harm you. You live in fear of what will happen when you inevitably mess up the next time.

The image of "Now You're Going to Get It God" develops when a child grows up in an environment where there is either subtle or overtly obvious abuse. You may have been the target of the abuse or may have watched as someone you cared about was bullied or abused. In this sort of environment, you live feeling terrified and violated without any sense of how to keep yourself or those you care about safe. You hear words that tear down rather than build up. Instead of receiving correction and guidance when you make mistakes, you are harshly punished in ways that communicate you are unlovable and incapable. The adults in your world become people you fear and move away from when you make mistakes instead of people who are safe and to whom you run for comfort and assistance. Your experience is one of living in a state of unpredictable danger, and this leaves you always looking for where you are going to be hurt next—both in your human relationships and in your relationship with God.

These summaries of common distortions of God make it easy to see how someone's faith could contribute to worry and anxiety. If I believe God is unpleasable or might abandon me at any time, it creates an underlying fear and anxiety I must constantly work to manage. Correcting our distorted understandings of God can help to eliminate this underlying worry so we can live with the calm, secure assurance we are loved by God, who will never leave us, will provide for us, and who cares deeply about every part of our lives. But how does this change occur?

As I have said before, factual memory cannot, in and of itself, change experiential memory. However, we need to know what the facts are before we can even know different experiences might be possible. Until there was evidence antibiotics might kill bacteria, no one even considered using this sort of medication when someone became ill and had a fever. Once there was evidence substances like penicillin might help people get better, someone still had to take the risk of experiencing whether this fact was true by taking the medication when they were ill and seeing if it helped them get better. This same thing is true in our relationship with God. While learning what Scripture says is true about God won't change the distortions we believe about God, it is a necessary starting point.

I started the chapter by sharing my distorted concept of God as someone who loved me but didn't like me. Instead of engaging in an intellectual battle with me to prove I was theologically inaccurate, the individual who asked the original question simply asked me what it meant that God loved me. I quoted "God is love" (1 John 4:8), to which the individual asked again, "What does this mean?" In the ensuing conversation, we concluded love is defined in 1 Corinthians 13 by a list of adjectives. The conversation ended there, but my mind would not rest. I took each of those adjectives and looked it up in the dictionary, starting with the word *patient.*

> Bearing pain or trial calmly or without complaint, manifesting forbearance under provocation or strain, not hasty or impetuous, steadfast despite opposition, difficulty, or adversity, able or willing to bear.[2]

Then I looked up synonyms for *patient.*

> Calm, forgiving, gentle, quiet, tolerant, long-suffering, understanding, accommodating, easygoing, enduring, even tempered, etc.[3]

Because I was starting to get just a bit uncomfortable about this time, I also looked up all the antonyms for *patient.*

> Agitated, loud, rough, troubled, violent, wild, frustrated, impatient, intolerant, unwilling, etc.[4]

I was now armed with a fairly complete, factual understanding of what it meant for love to be patient. The next step was to take this understanding and start allowing it to impact my experiences. I began by sitting with God and asking him to show me places where I had experienced things I thought were love or had been told were love but were not patient. To be honest, this felt incredibly wrong at first. I had to leave and come back to this process numerous times. Gradually, I composed a list of experiences I had defined as love but which could not be love if the definition included patience. I wrote about how each of those things felt and how it felt to own that these experiences were not love, even though I had defined them as love.

As you can tell, this took some time. The next part of the process was probably the scariest part for me, but it was necessary to create new experiences that replaced my unhealthy or inaccurate experiences. I began to own how I would like to experience God as patient and then asked him to show me how he was patient in those ways. One of the things I wrote was, "I want to feel like you aren't mad at me when I can't do things right the first time and have to practice before I can do something." Later the same day, I was reading a book explaining Colossians 1:22, "But now he has reconciled you by Christ's physical body through death to present you holy in his sight, without blemish and free from accusation." This book informed me that one way of translating this verse would be to say we stand before God as perfect, with nothing he can even chide us for. God having nothing to chide me for was inconceivable, and yet there it was in print. As I kept asking God to show me how this was true, he kept pointing out the ways I responded to my children when they made mistakes and were learning new things. I would tell them, "It's okay, let's try again." In my heart I would experience God saying, *If you are a flawed parent and that's how you respond to your children, why would you believe I would not perfectly do the same thing with you?*

I would like to say this process happened one time and my distorted concept of God was completely changed. However, nothing could be further from the truth. This was an incredibly intense process that took hours of studying what words meant and allowing God to provide experiences that brought those words alive in my life. I literally have a legal pad full of definitions, synonyms, antonyms, experiences, and requests of God. Over time, however, my concept of God has gradually shifted so I now believe he loves me *and* he likes me—even when I've messed up. I can't say my understanding is perfect, but I can say it is a core belief I can live out of the majority of the time.

As this shift occurred, the fear and anxiety in my life gradually calmed. I can tell when the old lie is rearing its ugly head because I begin to feel anxious and fearful I will make mistakes or lose God's approval.

While the experiences you need to change your distorted concept of God will, undoubtedly, be different from mine, there are some common components that are always present in the journey:

1. Define what the truth is by finding Scriptures to help you know what is true.

2. Own how your experiences as a child did not line up with this truth.

3. Process your experiences in a safe and validating environment where you can own your emotions, accurately label your experience, and forgive those who need to be forgiven.

4. Own how you would like to experience God differently than you have in the past.

5. Ask God to provide experiences of how he feels and acts toward you to bring this new understanding to life.

6. Take time each day to look for ways he is answering your request in real and tangible ways.

Consider keeping a written record of your journey so you can look back and see how you have grown and how God has shown himself to be a loving, dependable, caring, and patient being who understands what you are going through, cares about what you are going through, and is present in the midst of whatever you are experiencing.

CHAPTER SEVEN

STRATEGIES FOR DEALING WITH **WORRY AND ANXIETY**

L ooking at the biological, psychological, social, environmental, and spiritual factors is key to managing both worry and anxiety. When we work to address each of these areas in our life, we lessen the strain upon our body, mind, and spirit. However, some people can have significant stressors in all these areas of their life and yet are not plagued by worry and anxiety. Others find themselves battling with worry and anxiety every day without nearly as many factors affecting them. Why? Counselors, physicians, and researchers have spent years searching for the answer to this question. While we still don't have a complete answer, we are beginning to piece together some key differences between the two groups.

I want to start this section by reiterating there is no one cause and no one "cure" for either worry or anxiety. Both are the result of the complex interaction of all the factors we have discussed to this point. Having said this, when individuals who struggle with worry and anxiety are compared with those who face similar circumstances and don't struggle, a core set of skills begins to emerge as consistently being present in those who manage well emotionally. Exploring this has caused modern researchers to challenge some of the core tenets around which the fields of both psychology and education were originally based.

In the seventeenth century, philosopher John Locke took ideas from Aristotle and postulated that infants came into this world with minds that were a "tabula rasa," which has been translated to mean a blank slate.[1] He believed all minds were blank sheets of paper, and it was up to the environment around them to determine what they would become. Combine this with the fact that the only mechanism physicians at that time had for understanding the human brain was autopsy, and you get a very understandable working theory that all brains (just like all leg bones) are basically identical and function basically the same. Only what is experienced externally can then change how each brain functions. This understanding went largely unchallenged until the invention of the Functional MRI in 1990.

The Functional MRI provided researchers with the ability to see differences in how brains responded to various stimuli by measuring changes in blood flow to different areas of the brain in real time rather than simply at one moment in time (like a video rather than a picture). What researchers have discovered over time is that, while their basic structures look similar, individual brains are wired and respond very differently. As research into this area has expanded, it has become clear some people are born with brains that are highly sensitive and responsive to stimuli from the environment and the people around them.[2] Individuals born with sensitive brains are more aware of other people's emotions and can tend to personalize those emotions. They also tend to be more easily impacted and overwhelmed by environmental stimuli.

Imagine being an eighteen-month-old boy born with an emotionally sensitive brain to parents without such wiring. You start your day acutely aware of everything going on around you and, like all children, assume it is all about you. Your mother enters the kitchen worried about the presentation she must do at work, and suddenly you are overwhelmed with anxiety—you feel what she is feeling and you assume she is feeling this about you. Your father is late for work and shoots through the kitchen on his way to the garage without taking time to acknowledge you. You are overwhelmed with sadness and a sense of abandonment. Throughout the day, you are intensely aware of your emotions and the emotions of everyone around you, to the point that you are aware of almost nothing else. That night, you awaken scared by a bad dream—but you are not just scared like your siblings, you are terrified. Your parents groggily reassure you that you are fine and do not understand why you won't just settle down and go back to sleep. Your parents, without knowing you are not wired like they are, assume you have the skills needed to manage the level of distress a non–emotionally sensitive brain would be experiencing. They are quickly frustrated by what seems to be your unwillingness to calm down and go back to sleep. Assuming this is willfulness rather than inability, they remind you big boys aren't afraid of the dark and you are making inappropriate choices by refusing to obey their directive to go back to sleep. They then leave you in your room to get yourself under control and go back to sleep. The problem is, your fear was overwhelming to start with. It has now been compounded by your acute sensitivity to their frustration with you and your perception they have abandoned you. You didn't have the skills needed to calm yourself when you woke afraid, and you certainly don't have the skills to calm yourself when your parents leave. Left in the flood of your emotions, you will either cry inconsolably for hours or your body will become so emotionally overwhelmed you will disconnect from your emotions and shut down, neither of which are helpful. Children born with more sensitive brains often have experiences like this—not just one day but every day.

Children who are wired to be more emotionally sensitive experience more intense emotions than other children. These intense emotions frequently overwhelm their skills and leave them feeling out of control. Also, because they are so consumed by their emotional experiences, they are not able to focus on and learn skills other children their age are learning. Much of what we learn about how to manage emotions is learned by watching those around us, picking up on what they are doing, and mimicking it in our own lives. Children who are more emotionally sensitive can be so consumed by what they are experiencing, they are unaware of what others are doing to cope. Thus, they don't naturally pick up on the skills their peers are learning. This leaves these children with more intense emotions, less validation from others for what they are feeling, and fewer skills with which to manage their emotions.

Armed with this new information, the field of psychology has begun to recognize the need to teach skills for managing emotions. These are skills many individuals grow up learning simply by being around parents, teachers, and peers. They can also be deliberately taught to help manage emotions—including anxiety. In the next section of this book, we will explore three of these skills I have found to be particularly important for individuals struggling with anxiety. Dr. Marsha Linehan has researched what happens when individuals are deliberately taught these skills and found they effectively help individuals increase their ability to regulate emotions and tolerate distressing situations.[3] We will not go through all the skills Dr. Linehan determined can be helpful, but we will explore:

1. what it means to stay grounded in and live fully present in the current moment
2. how to suspend judgment and work to accept ourselves, our circumstances, and others exactly where they are

3. ways to see ourselves as competent to manage distressing emotions when they occur so we do not need to avoid them and can find contentment in the current moment

Let me set the stage for why these skills are so important by using the Israelites of the Old Testament as our example.

In the book of Exodus, the Israelites have been held in captivity for years—through no fault of their own—much like many people I know have been held captive by anxiety for much of their lives. God promised to rescue them and sent a leader who had his own anxiety issues. (Moses initially refused when God asked him to go because he didn't speak well and wasn't sure what he would say.) After God miraculously parted the Red Sea for the Israelites to walk through on dry land and killed the Egyptians when they tried to follow, the Israelites found themselves in the desert. They were free from the Egyptians but had no idea how to live in this freedom—perhaps just as you can't comprehend what it would be like to live without the tyranny of anxiety in your life.

Fast-forward a few days and the Israelites began to experience hunger. They cried out, "If only we had died by the Lord's hand in Egypt! There we sat around pots of meat and ate all the food we wanted, but you have brought us out into this desert to starve this entire assembly to death" (Exod. 16:3). God's answer: manna. God was working to teach them. They could trust him. He was clear they were only going to get what they needed for the day they were in—no more, no less. Some of the Israelites were still not sure they could trust God and were fearful of not having what they needed for tomorrow. They attempted to make sure they would be taken care of by collecting enough manna for more than one day (even though God told them not to do this). The result: the manna rotted. God promised to give them what they needed for each day, on that day, not ahead of time. When they attempted to take the things they were given for the day and use them for the future, it didn't work. The same is true when we jump into the future and attempt to use the resources God has given us for today to solve problems we believe might occur in the future; it never works successfully and frequently spoils the moment we are currently in.

God provided manna and promised the Israelites it would fulfill their nutritional needs. He promised they had everything they needed to be competent and content during their trek to the promised land. The Israelites, however, had not learned to see themselves as capable of handling things that were not exactly the way they believed they should be. They consistently believed they needed something not currently present in order to be okay. Thus, they were satisfied by the manna for a time but then began to be discontented with what they had and were distressed by having to deal with the same food every day. Instead of handling this discomfort, they struggled to manage their emotions, and in Numbers 11 they announced, "If only we had meat to eat! We remember the fish we ate in Egypt at no cost—also the cucumbers, melons, leeks, onions and garlic. But now we have lost our appetite; we never see anything but this manna!" (vv. 4–6). They judged the present moment, judged God, and predicted the future instead of living in the present moment. Their demand for something other than what they had created even more distress in their current moment.

Having safely delivered them from the Egyptians and provided them with food and water, God next asked the Israelites to wait while Moses went up the mountain to get instructions on how to live in this new freedom. At first they were fine, but it didn't take long for them to begin to get anxious. Mind you, they were fine in the present moment. They had food. They had water. They were in no danger. Their anxiety came from worrying about what might happen in the future. They started to worry . . .

What if Moses doesn't come back . . .

What if God leaves us here . . .

What if we are attacked . . .

We need a leader . . .

We need food . . .

We need . . .

Their inability to stay in the moment they were currently in and see themselves as competent to handle their circumstances because they were in the hands of a competent God, who would give them what they needed, led them to seek a way out of their distress—thus they made a golden calf to worship instead of God. Their desire to find a way out of their anxiety about what might happen in the future and their judgment that they had been abandoned by both Moses and God led them to engage in behaviors that were destructive. Sound like anything you might ever be inclined to do?

Next, they arrived at the Jordan River to cross over into what God had promised them would be a "land flowing with milk and honey" (Lev. 20:24). However, they didn't see themselves as competent and capable, led and empowered by God, to enter this new land, conquer those inhabiting the land, and establish a new life. Instead, they started trying to figure out if they had what it would take by sending out spies. This gave them a lot of data that was terrifying and started a whole new litany of "what ifs." They operated out of the fear of what might happen combined with the assumption they wouldn't have what they needed because they didn't currently have it. This resulted in an additional forty years of wandering in the wilderness.

By the time they arrived back at the Jordan River forty years later, they had learned some different skills and were better equipped to trust they would be able, with God's leading and empowerment, to cross over and take the land. This was remarkable, given they didn't have any more physical resources with them at the moment they stepped into the Jordan River than they had forty years earlier. Having the skills to manage their emotions and suspend judgment about what might happen allowed them to trust they would have what they needed when they stepped into the Jordan and waited expectantly for God to part the water.

Just as the Israelites learned new skills and a new ability to trust God to provide what they needed to be competent, each of us can learn the skills necessary to manage our emotions and operate within our current environment in a competent manner, even if our circumstances are not the ones we would wish for. In the next four chapters, we will explore what is encompassed in each of these skills, as well as ways these skills can be developed and implemented.

CHAPTER EIGHT

LIVING IN THE PRESENT MOMENT

B y the time I arrived at work this morning, I had been awake for over two hours. However, I had little actual awareness of what had happened in those two hours. I showered while thinking (okay, obsessing) about what I was going to wear to work and have for breakfast, so I honestly don't remember washing my hair or anything else I did while I was in the shower. While I was cooking and eating breakfast, I was also packing my lunch and my computer bag for work, leaving me with no awareness of how my food looked, smelled, or tasted. I spent the thirty-minute drive to work finishing my breakfast and planning ways to accomplish all the tasks I felt I needed to complete that day while resisting the urge to check email on my phone while driving. I wish I could say once I arrived at work all of this stopped, I became tuned in to the moment I was in, and I was aware of God's presence in that moment. However, unless I consciously work at keeping my mind focused on the present moment, I can spend my entire day doing exactly what I did during those first two hours . . . living my life unaware of the present and consumed by what needs to happen in the future or what has happened in the past.

Does any of this resonate with you? Most of us have learned to live our lives largely unaware of the moment we are currently in because we are consumed by the future and the past. However, this is not how we were created to function. Jesus tells us we aren't supposed to worry about our future.

> Therefore I tell you, do not worry about your life, what you will eat or drink; or about your body, what you will wear. Is not life more than food, and the body more than clothes? Look at the birds of the air; they do not sow or reap or store away in barns, and yet your heavenly Father feeds them. Are you not much more valuable than they? Can any one of you by worrying add a single hour to your life?
>
> And why do you worry about clothes? See how the flowers of the field grow. They do not labor or spin. Yet I tell you that not even Solomon in all his splendor was dressed like one of these. If that is how God clothes the grass of the field, which is here today and to-morrow is thrown into the fire, will he not much more clothe you—you of little faith? So do not worry, saying, "What shall we eat?" or "What shall we drink?" or "What shall we wear?" For the pagans run after all these things, and your heavenly Father knows that you need them. But seek first his kingdom and his righteousness, and all these things will be given to you as well. Therefore do not worry about tomorrow, for tomorrow will worry about itself. Each day has enough trouble of its own. (Matt. 6:25–34)

While I would like to say I was "planning" instead of worrying this morning, the truth is I worried about what to wear, I worried about how to do my day right, I worried about what was in the emails I hadn't read or responded to yet, and I worried about what the people who wrote those emails might be thinking about me and my lack of response. When I am focused on these things, I am unable to be aware of God's gift of the present moment.

Worry and anxiety are rarely about what is going on in the present. Both are focused on what might happen or what has happened in the past. Luckily, this focus on the future or the past is a learned habit, not something we are born with. I have never seen an infant or toddler worried about the future or the past. In fact, when my children were toddlers, they would become so immersed in what they were doing as they played that they were unaware of their need to go to the bathroom or anything else. They were totally tuned in to what was happening in the present moment and blissfully unaware of anything else going on. However, those same children, by the time they were in elementary school, had learned to fret and worry about what was going to be served for supper, when they were going to get to play with their friends, and who might be mad at them on the playground that day.

Worrying or being anxious about the future increases our sense of powerlessness. While I was driving my car to work, there was absolutely nothing I could do about any of the things I was worrying about. I couldn't take any actions to fix the problems, I couldn't answer the emails, I couldn't change what people thought of me. So I spent my thirty-minute drive thinking about things I had no power to change. This, in turn, decreased my awareness of the things in the present moment I did have the ability to influence and change. When we live consumed by the future or the past, we are less aware of what is happening in the present and less able to react effectively within the moment.

As I have alluded to previously, God has consistently utilized the Israelites to teach me about myself and how he functions with me. How to live in the present moment is one of the lessons I learned from the Israelites. When the Israelites were traveling in the desert between Egypt and the promised land, God promised he would provide for them. He told them manna would be present each morning and they were to go out and gather what they needed for the day. He explicitly told them he would give them what they needed for the day each morning, and he would not give them what they needed for tomorrow. When the Israelites tried to keep the manna overnight so they could use it the next day, it spoiled and wasn't usable.

God wants an intimate relationship with us where we come to him and receive from him what we need as we need it. He doesn't want a relationship where we show up once a week, or even once a day, to get a shopping cart full of what we will need and then come back for a refill when we have used up those resources.

When I am worrying about the future, I am attempting to figure out how to handle something in two minutes, two hours, or two days with the resources God has given me to handle the moment I am currently in. This will never work, because the resources for this moment will always be insufficient to address what I need in any other moment. Just like the Israelites had to learn to trust that God would give them what they needed, we must learn to trust in God's provision. This trust can only be learned by experience . . . the experience of being in the present moment and recognizing God's presence and provision in the present moment. To do this, we must relearn the skills we used when we were young—before we learned to worry. When these skills are utilized consistently, they make us aware of God's presence with us in the present moment, his provision for us, and his Spirit empowering us to do what he has called us to in this moment. When we are aware of ourselves and God's presence in the present moment, we experience both more fully.

Take in the Moment

God created us with five senses. These senses only give us data about what is going on in the current moment. The things we can see, hear, feel, touch, and taste are things from the current moment. When we calm our mind and focus it on the things we can sense, it brings us back to the current moment. Take a minute and try it. Sit comfortably and find a place to fix your gaze. Without moving anything (including your eyes), what are five things you can see? What are five things you can hear? What are five things you feel (both physically and emotionally)? What are five things you are touching? You may also want to be aware of anything you can taste, although this might be harder if you aren't chewing gum or eating something.

During the time it took you to do this activity, you were more aware of what was present in the moment you were currently in. While you were doing this, you were probably not focused on anything else, which means you had to let go of worry thoughts for at least a moment. Law enforcement officials spend a lot of time learning to be aware of their surroundings. This awareness helps them to stay safe and to be aware of situations where they need to intervene. Dancers and musicians must be aware of the music to the point they let go of everything else and are only aware of the music and their bodies. When they do this, they respond to the music in ways that produce amazing works of art.

When I engage in this activity, I often find myself with a heightened awareness of my surroundings. For example, when I drive to work aware of the current moment, I am more mindful of the beauty of the sunrise, the beauty of the landscape around me, and of myself as I sit in my car. Focusing on these things is calming.

In addition to having five physical senses, you are also a spiritual being, which means you can sense God's presence. When you take time to calm and center yourself, your spirit can also become centered and more aware of God's presence with you.

Give Language to the Moment

Your senses help to bring you into the current moment and make you aware of what is in it. The information we take in when we

121

use our senses to be aware of the moment enters our brain through the limbic system. The limbic system takes in the data and creates an emotional, instinctual response to this data.

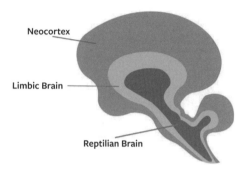

You may have heard the limbic system referred to as part of the reptilian complex or the reptilian brain. Technically, the limbic system is folded over what was originally considered the reptilian brain: the basal ganglia, cerebral cortex, and brain stem, which are responsible for the autonomic responses within our body (breathing, heart rate, digestion, pupil response, urination, body temperature, and balance). The limbic system is responsible for instinctual responses that can occur without conscious thinking: fight, flight, freeze, fear, feeding, and reproducing. When you put the activities of the limbic system, basal ganglia, cerebral cortex, and brain stem together, you get the activities reptiles are capable of—thus the name. Left on its own, the limbic system only has those six options to utilize in response to the data coming in through our senses. Fortunately, God created us with more than a limbic system within our brains.

When the sensory system sends signals to our brain, we can engage in activities that help our brain to interpret the data it is receiving. This requires engaging other parts of the brain, and one way to do this is to begin the process of accurately labeling the information we are observing.

When I see an expression on my friend's face and feel fear as a response, I am reacting to lots of sensory data instantaneously without the need to think through things first. Fear (often another word for anxiety) is a powerful emotion and, when I see my friend's face and experience fear, I will want to respond by fighting, fleeing, or freezing. However, those three reactions are not my only options. If I am willing to slow down, observe what is happening in the current moment, and then actively begin to describe what it is I am observing, more options will begin to emerge for me to choose from.

When we describe the data observed through our senses, we begin to give language to our experience. Research has shown attaching words to sensory experiences decreases the response of the amygdala (responsible for fight, flight, or freeze) and increases activity in the ventrolateral prefrontal cortex.[1] The ventrolateral prefrontal cortex is the part of the brain associated with suppressing instinctual responses and making choices that help us to accomplish our goals.[2] To begin giving language to something requires two things:

1. Having words that accurately describe what you are observing.
2. Only giving language to what is actually present.

While both seem simple and easily attainable, in reality they can be rather difficult at times.

Having Words

As someone who talks with people all day and enjoys writing, it is not particularly difficult for me to find words to describe the desk I am sitting at. It is an off-white color with a simulated wood pattern, about forty-two inches long, and is located in front of a window overlooking a frozen drainage pond. Engaging in the process of writing this last sentence caused me to focus my attention and think of words that fit my experience. It made me more aware of my desk and the view from my window, which increased my appreciation of both. However, this is not an easy thing for many people to do—especially if what is being described is an emotion and the person attempting to describe it is male.

We are born as feeling little beings totally reliant upon the adults in our world to help us both identify and manage what we are feeling. This process of learning to label what we are feeling involves having the adults in our world validate what we are feeling and then give us labels for these feelings. As a two-year-old, my son cried every day when I dropped him off at daycare on my way to work. You can probably imagine how difficult this was for both of us. I had to work and needed to be on time, so I felt intense guilt and sadness mingled with swirls of fear and anger every time he burst into tears and clung to my leg. I felt guilty for leaving him at daycare, sad he was distressed, and simultaneously afraid I wasn't going to be competent enough as a mother to calm him so I could gracefully exit and get to school on time. Anger was a well-honed coping strategy I used to deal with feelings I didn't like, so it cropped up to mask my fear—both from myself and from anyone looking in.

My son, on the other hand, felt intense fear and anxiety as I sat him down and prepared to walk out the door. He had experiences in his short life that told him sometimes people left and never came back. He felt out of control and afraid. He also has a sensitive brain so he felt things intensely and had difficulty knowing how to regulate these intense emotions.

For me to parent effectively, I needed to be able to observe, accurately describe, and appropriately manage my emotions while simultaneously validating his emotions, labeling his emotions for him, and helping him to manage his emotions. Easy-peasy, right? I wish I could tell you all my years of college equipped me to effectively help him own, label, and manage his feelings. Unfortunately, more days than not, I struggled to manage my own emotions and, in the process, often minimized, discounted, and ignored his emotions. This left him without permission to have his feelings, words to describe his feelings, or tools to calm himself.

My son, like most American men, grew up learning from the culture around him that "big boys" didn't cry, weren't sad, and weren't afraid. American culture teaches men they can be either happy or angry. This leaves them with a lot of emotions and only two categories to put them in. Thus, many men have a difficult time describing themselves as anything other than fine, happy, or angry. Without words to label their emotional experiences, their ability to shift from being driven by their amygdala to engaging their whole brain is compromised. While this may be more stereotypically true of men, anyone raised in an environment where the adults around them did not validate and appropriately label their emotions lacks the words essential to move out of being held captive by the reactions of their limbic system.

If this describes you, the first step is to begin finding words for what you are experiencing. The appendix at the back of this book contains a list of feeling words. As you go through the list, take time to look up what the words mean and then watch for places in your life where the definition fits. Over time, you will begin to teach yourself how to identify and accurately label what you are feeling. Another important activity is to begin verifying what other people are feeling. Instead of assuming they are either happy or angry, ask them what they are feeling. This allows you to begin appropriately labeling the things you are observing instead of assuming you know what they are. While this is especially important if you grew up without learning to label feelings, it is important within all relationships. We tend to assume we know what someone else is feeling without checking it out. Many times we are incredibly wrong. Marital conflict, for example, would be significantly reduced if we were willing to inquisitively ask our partner what they are experiencing instead of assuming the worst or telling them what they are feeling.

Only Describing What Is Actually Present

If we go back to my experience of my friend's face that provoked me to fear, I would probably describe what I saw as "angry face." However, that is not necessarily what was present; it was the story I created out of the data I observed. What I actually observed might sound more like this: my friend had her eyebrows furrowed, her lips pursed, and her hands on her hips. Simply describing those pieces of data instead of using the words "angry face" would prompt my amygdala to calm some. This would allow other parts of my brain to kick in and attempt to determine what is happening and how I should respond to best accomplish my goals, both now and in my life overall.

If this is the only data I observe and describe, I may still be left fearful that my friend is angry. However, if I expand what I am aware of by looking beyond her face to other things around her, I begin to push back against the tunnel vision that occurs when my amygdala reacts in fear. What if I also saw her brown, floppy-eared Yorkshire terrier sitting in front of her, its head cocked to one side, with one of her black dress shoes hanging out of its mouth? Even reading these words probably changed your internal experience; it would certainly change my experience in the moment. For me, my fear would be replaced by a desire to giggle as I anticipate my friend engaging in some sort of friendly tussle with her pet to rescue her shoe. What was your internal reaction as you read my description? Our reactions are based upon our previous experiences and our values. This makes it important to keep being very present in the moment and working to give language to the moment without creating a story and treating this story as though it is a fact.

Since our brains are "meaning making machines," we are constantly creating stories to explain the data our senses take in. Sometimes these stories are helpful because they allow us to assess rapidly what is happening and what we need to do in response. However, worry or anxiety can easily distort the meaning our brains make of the data it is taking in. For example, if I am in my dorm room enjoying a relaxing evening watching tv and I hear a door bang somewhere down the hall, I will probably think very little of it and go on with my tv show. However, what if the door bangs when I am worried about whether I am going to pass my exam in the morning, my hands are sweaty, my heart is racing, and I am having trouble focusing on the tv show? In all likelihood, I am going to physically react by being startled as a jolt of adrenaline courses through my body. My brain will be more apt to conclude something negative is happening in the hallway and I am in danger simply because I was already anxious. In both instances, however, the only thing that happened was a door banging.

Having a feeling or a thought does not mean the feeling or thought is a fact. The entire next chapter will be spent exploring how to slow down your brain, stop telling stories, and differentiate between feelings and facts. For now, it is important to be aware that the goal is to describe only what you can take in using your senses and to do so as accurately as possible. The act of working to describe things slows down your amygdala and helps you make better choices.

Throw Yourself into the Moment

Being aware of what is happening in the current moment and giving language to what you observe makes you more present in the moment. The next step is to let go and fully participate in the moment. I described the first few hours of my day at the beginning of this chapter. I definitely was not throwing myself into those moments and fully experiencing them! Instead, I was going through the motions while thinking about something else entirely—you know, multitasking, being efficient, using my time wisely. Sounds plausible, right? The only problem with my explanation is research consistently shows attempting to multitask doesn't make us more efficient.[3] In fact, we may lose up to 40 percent of our productivity when we attempt to multitask.[4] Our brains were not designed to multitask, and when we attempt to do so, we are simply not able to be very effective at either task.

Worrying or being anxious requires us to be either unaware or only partially aware of the moment we are currently in. Worry is not about the current moment. It requires us to split our attention between what is actually happening and what we are anxious about. When we choose to fully participate in the thing we are currently doing or the one moment we are currently in, it invites us to let go of worried, anxious thoughts and fully experience what is actually happening.

Many of us are acutely aware of our anxious thoughts and feelings. We throw ourselves into these thoughts and feelings to the exclusion of what is actually happening around us. Thus, it is very important to choose carefully what we throw ourselves into. If the thoughts and feelings you are currently experiencing are distressing or are not helping you to accomplish your current goal, it becomes important to become aware of what is going on externally, give language to it, and fully engage with it. For example, I was recently in a meeting with several important leaders and found myself on the edge of tears and feeling very anxious. The more I told myself this was not a good time to cry, the closer I felt myself creeping to tears. Generally speaking, the more you tell yourself not to feel something, the more the emotion intensifies and demands your attention. Instead of attempting not to cry, I chose to become very focused on what was happening externally. I started by focusing on the physical feeling of my bottom on the chair and then moved to focusing on the eyebrows and hair of the leader currently speaking. As I focused on these things, the lump in my throat faded from my awareness. I continued to watch the way the marker wrote on the board as the group leader expounded on her point and counted the times she shifted from one foot to another until I was no longer on the verge of tears and could re-engage in the conversation.

You can use this same strategy if you are feeling anxious or panicky. Instead of focusing on how anxious you feel, use the activity you practiced earlier in the chapter and shift your focus to what you can see, hear, feel, touch, and even taste. I have my clients fix their eyes in one location and then describe five things they can see, five things they can hear, and five things they can physically feel. Without repeating their answers or moving their head, they then describe four things they can see, four things they can hear, and four things they can physically feel, and repeat until they are down to one thing they can see, hear, and feel. If, at the end of this exercise, they are still feeling anxious, I ask them to switch where they are looking and repeat the exercise. Sometimes this can avert a panic attack and, even if it doesn't, it will help you "ride the wave" of the panic until it subsides.

Sometimes the distress is related to what is happening around you, not what is happening within you. Let's say you are at a Christmas gathering and total chaos reigns: wrapping paper is everywhere, children are crying, the adults are yelling at one another about who should have done things differently, and you can't politely excuse yourself to get out of the situation. This would be an ideal time to shift your focus from being aware of what is happening externally to focusing on what is happening internally. Survey your body and be aware of what you are feeling in your toes, in your arms, in your stomach. Follow your breath in and feel your chest fill and then be aware of the feel of the air as it leaves your nose when you exhale. Tense up your legs and your toes and tune in to how this feels and then release the tension and notice what changes. By moving inward and being aware of what is happening in your body, you can participate in this experience and let go of participating in the chaos around you.

We can choose whether we focus on an internal or external moment, but we can't always keep our attention focused where we would like it to be. Whether you are working to focus on counting the ceiling tiles while a nurse inserts an IV or you are focusing on relaxing the tension in your shoulders while your teenager yells that you are an awful parent, your attention will likely not stay where you want it to be. This is normal! Learning to control where we are focusing our attention and what we are participating in is a skill that takes practice to develop. When you find your mind moving, distracted from the present moment, or focusing on distressing parts of the present moment, see this as normal. When your mind becomes distracted, gently refocus on whatever it is you are working to participate in.

You may find yourself needing to refocus multiple times but, over time, your skill at being aware of the present moment, giving language to the present moment, and throwing yourself into the present moment will grow. You can grow your skill by practicing even when you are not anxious or worried. Tomorrow, when you go through your morning routine, work to be fully aware of every task involved, give good descriptive language to what you are doing and how it feels to do these things, and see if you can throw yourself into each part of getting ready for your day. By practicing on the daily tasks of your life, you will enjoy your life more and build the skills you need to effectively stop worry and anxiety from robbing you of this experience.

Building This Skill

Below are five activities you can use to practice building this skill. By planning each of these five activities into your week and repeating them weekly, over time they will become a natural part of your life. As this happens, you will be able to access the skills even when you are in stressful and anxiety provoking situations. Start by doing them in situations that are not anxiety provoking so you have the mental and emotional energy necessary to learn something new.

1. Pick an activity you do daily—something like making lunch, going for a walk, petting the dog, or talking with your spouse—and work to be very aware of everything that happens during the activity. Don't try to describe it or evaluate how well it went or anything like that. Just see if you can be totally present in the moment and observe what is happening in the moment. What did you see, hear, feel, touch, and taste?

2. Pick a feeling you are experiencing—angry, anxious, happy, sad—and work to only be aware of everything associated with experiencing this emotion. Be aware of all the physical feelings you have in your stomach, shoulders, fingers, back, and other parts of your body as you experience this emotion. What are the thoughts you hear in your head associated with this feeling? Does anything change about what you see or feel externally as a result of this emotion? Remember, the goal is to observe every aspect of this feeling, not evaluate whether you should be feeling it or make sure you have the right language.

3. While you are eating something you enjoy, work to describe the experience of eating. What do you see connected to eating? What do you hear both externally and

internally as you eat? What does the substance feel like in your mouth? What does the utensil feel like in your hand? What do you smell? What are the tastes? Work to give language to each and every aspect of eating. What happened as you worked to do this?

4. Pick an activity you might normally "go through the motions" to accomplish—something like folding the laundry or putting gas in the car—and work to throw yourself fully into doing this activity. Let yourself be unaware of anything other than completing this activity. Work to observe and describe every aspect of what you are doing. If your mind wants to wander, gently bring it back to what you are doing in this present moment.

5. As you are doing something routine, allow yourself to focus on God's presence with you as you complete this activity. God is everywhere and in everything. He is breathing the breath into your lungs right now. You are surrounded by him and enfolded in his loving arms right this minute, no matter what you are doing. Allow yourself to be aware that you are being empowered by him to complete this task in this moment. He is giving you what you need to accomplish this, he is delighting in you as you accomplish this, and he is working with you to accomplish this.

CHAPTER NINE

LETTING GO of JUDGMENT

This week I was slated to present a workshop on dealing effectively with stress to an organization about two and one-half hours away from my office. I hopped into the car two and three-quarter hours prior to the presentation, loaded the address into my GPS, set out on the back roads required to get to my intended destination, and answered a phone call on my cell. About thirty minutes into the drive, as I continued conducting business via my phone, I suddenly noticed a sign announcing the next town was coming up in eight miles. A wave of fear coursed through my body as I read the sign. The town identified on the sign was not anywhere near where I should be—in fact, it was west of where I had started, and my intended destination was east of where I had started. I glanced at my GPS while talking on the phone (so much for doing one thing at a time and being fully present in the one thing I'm doing) and quickly realized it was no longer connected to whatever satellite it got information from and was "searching." I was now more than twenty minutes off-course in the wrong direction. My technical difficulties meant I was now going to be at least fifteen minutes late instead of fifteen minutes early.

Realistically, this truly wasn't a big deal: no one was dead or injured, I still had the ability to get from where I was to where I needed to go, and I had the contact information for the individual coordinating the event so I could call her and give her two hours' advance warning. However, none of these facts were driving the narrative in my head. The moment I realized I was not where I belonged, the litany began: *Oh my goodness, how could you have let this happen? You are such an idiot! You know better than to trust the GPS, and you should have written the directions out on paper. If you had been paying attention, you would have known the GPS wasn't working and you would have seen the turn. How could you have missed a turn? You have driven this route tons of times, and you should have noticed.* I wish I could tell you it stopped there, but it didn't.

I called the event organizer and apologized profusely even though she graciously reassured me numerous times it wasn't a big deal and would be fine. After I hung up with her, the tirade in my head shifted. *She's ticked at me. I know she thinks I'm an idiot because I can't even get there on time. I've made a mess of her day. She's never going to want me to come back and speak again. They think I'm an incompetent moron, and if I can't be trusted to get there on time, there is no way they are going to trust anything else I have to say. How am I ever going to get through this?*

I was now deep into the worry zone, filled with dread, and frustrated with every slow driver in front of me, even though there was no way any of them were making me any later than I already was. The irony of driving to do a presentation on stress management while worrying and stressing myself out was not lost on me. It took me the next entire hour to halt the litany of self-criticism in my head and relax my body enough that I wasn't white-knuckle driving while announcing to the empty air in my car that "People need to learn to drive!" every time I encountered a driver not obsessed with getting to their destination as fast as possible.

While I wish this situation was an anomaly in my life, more times than I would like this is my reaction when things don't go the way I believe they should. It is a habit as engrained as tying my shoes or brushing my teeth, so it happens without my conscious awareness much of the time.

In his Sermon on the Mount, Jesus admonished his audience, "Do not judge, or you too will be judged. For in the same way you judge others, you will be judged, and with the measure you use, it will be measured to you" (Matt. 7:1–2). It would be hard to find people—whether Christian or non-Christian—who don't believe Jesus's teaching here represents wisdom. Most of us want to be nonjudgmental, loving individuals. So, if we know judging is something we shouldn't do because it is hurtful to both ourselves and others, why do we keep doing it? Why was my response to making a mistake judging myself, assuming others were judging me, and proceeding to judge everyone around me for not doing what I wanted them to do?

In the Garden of Eden, Adam and Eve were told not to eat from the tree of the knowledge of good and evil (synonyms for right and wrong). They were told the result would be death. Satan showed up and tempted them to believe learning to judge right from wrong wouldn't kill them but, rather, would give them the ability to do what they currently had to trust God to do for them. Until this time, they had trusted God to tell them what was right and what was wrong. God's job was to judge. Their job was to trust he loved them with all his heart, was taking care of them, and would guide them through whatever life held for them.

God—who loved Adam and Eve and wanted them to live forever walking in the garden with him, perfectly basking in his lavish love for them and perfectly loving one another—told them they could eat from any tree except for one—the tree of the knowledge of good and evil. Until recently, I had never really thought much about this command. However, if there was only one tree they were forbidden to eat from, this means they had been given permission to eat from the tree of life. Studying this passage and studying what is present in the lives of emotionally and physically healthy individuals reveals strikingly similar results: we were created to thrive when we feast upon things that bring life but to die when our lives are filled with attempting to determine what is right (good) and what is wrong (evil).

My initial reaction when I began contemplating this concept was similar to what happens when I bring this up with my clients. An incredulous voice in my head cried, *But we can't just do whatever we want!* and this is also the almost unanimous protest I hear from my clients. It is also absolutely and unequivocally true! We can't do whatever we want and expect to have a healthy life. However, we also don't have to spend our lives judging. Judging doesn't make our lives healthy and full. If my life is to be oriented around what brings life, I must be tuned in and aware of what brings life to me and to others in any given situation. What brings life to me when I am five won't be the same as what brings life to me when I'm fifty-five. What brings life to me also won't always be the same as what brings life to my best friend.

Not only do I need to be tuned in to God and to what brings life in any given situation but I also must be willing to make sure I am engaging in those things in both the short and long term. Being aware of what will bring life to me and to others requires an intimate connection with God—the source of all life and the one who promises to lead us in ways that bring life. Out of this intimate connection with God, I can then approach the situations in my life by asking myself and God, "What will produce life in this situation?"

We were not created to judge. When we engage in the process of attempting to figure out what is right and wrong, it creates fear and anxiety that kill our ability to live connected to and trusting God and also cripples our ability to live in freedom. The anxiety this creates has been scientifically proven to shorten our lives. Scripture is 100 percent correct when it says judgment leads to death. Since this is the case, it seems important to understand what judgment is, how it creates anxiety, and what steps we can take to suspend judgment and live a nonjudgmental life.

What Is Judgment?

Judgment can be defined as an opinion, an estimation, a belief, an idea, thoughts about something, or a criticism.[1] Using this definition helps us know what is involved in judging. Forming a judgment involves taking a group of facts (my GPS lost its connection, I didn't notice right away, I drove on a road going west for twenty minutes though my destination was to the east, etc.) and forming an opinion about those facts (I was being an idiot, anyone would have known better, the event organizer was angry and wouldn't want me back, etc.). Simply put, judgment is turning my opinions, ideas, or beliefs into facts and then acting upon my judgments as though they are facts. The facts I listed above don't really have an emotional charge, and I need to be aware of those facts so I can make good and healthy decisions about what to do next. However, the judgments I created from those facts *are* emotionally charged. They are also totally unnecessary for making healthy decisions and often make it very difficult to make wise decisions about next steps. Knowing my GPS had lost its connection and I was now twenty minutes west of where I needed to be caused me to reset my GPS and turn around. Telling myself I was an idiot who should have known better, was no longer respected, and was no longer seen as competent by my audience created intense feelings of fear and incompetence, making it difficult to form thoughts or make healthy decisions.

Why Do We Judge?

If judgment creates emotional pain, fills us with anxiety, and makes it hard to be effective, why do we do it? While I'm sure there are many reasons, they can often be lumped into three main categories: protection, control, and motivation.

We Think Judging Will Protect Us

The habit of judging develops when we are young and think in very concrete terms. When our parents got upset and scolded us for walking through the house wearing our muddy boots, our little brains heard we *were* bad, and we felt unloved. Toddlers often can't cognitively comprehend that someone good can make bad choices or someone making bad choices can be loved. Feeling bad and unlovable is such an uncomfortable feeling that we are highly motivated to avoid it or protect ourselves from it in every way possible. In our toddler brains, it seemed as though being able to predict when this feeling was going to show up would help us to be ready for it and protect ourselves from it. If we could determine when Mom was going to be upset with us for doing something wrong, we could then steel ourselves against the feelings this would bring and minimize these feelings so they didn't feel as intolerable.

Fast-forward fifty years to me driving in the wrong direction and my subsequent internal dialogue. If I predict all the different ways people might be upset with me and all the ways they might reject me prior to walking into the presentation, I feel as though I have armed myself so their arrows of disapproval and rejection won't hurt quite so much. While this might seem effective, in reality it is like hitting your finger with a hammer repeatedly just in case you slam it in the car door later. No one would volunteer to hit their finger with a hammer to prepare themselves for the potential it might get slammed in a door. However, we engage in the emotional equivalent of this daily when we berate ourselves with the things we are fearful others might think and feel about us in an attempt to make sure we are prepared and protected if it happens.

We Think Judging Will Give Us Control

Back in the garden of Eden, when Satan tempted Adam and Eve, his temptation was that God didn't want them to learn right and wrong because he wanted to keep Adam and Eve from being like him and having control. We, like Adam and Eve, don't really like being dependent on others or having things we didn't expect happen to us. We want to be firmly in the driver's seat of our lives and able to successfully predict what is going to happen so we can be prepared for things or prevent them from ever happening. We don't want to feel dependent on others, and we don't want to ever find ourselves in a situation where we might not have everything necessary to get what we want.

Ultimately, we have constructed a picture in our head of how things "should" go and believe that if we can judge what everyone and everything will do, we will be able to control all the variables and the picture will come out the way we believe it should. If you have ever seen a young woman turn into a "bridezilla," you have seen this in action. Such brides are notorious for making elaborate plans in their heads about how their wedding "should" go and then attempting to micromanage everyone and everything to make it happen. As long as everyone and everything cooperates with her internal picture of what she has judged a perfect wedding to be, all is well. However, the minute a bridesmaid has the wrong hue of fingernail polish or some other detail is wrong, the meltdown begins. The bride's judgment of what "should" be is an attempt to control everyone and everything so she can obtain a desired outcome—whether or not it is realistic. Unfortunately, when the world doesn't cooperate, her emotions spin out of control just like our worry and anxiety spin out of control when life doesn't go the way we judge it "ought" to go.

We Think Judging Will Motivate Either Us or Others

Often, if you ask me why I allowed the judgmental litany to unleash itself in my head, I would tell you it motivates me to do things differently or better. While it is true human beings are motivated to move away from painful stimuli, it is equally true humans are *more* motivated to move toward pleasurable stimuli. Additionally, moving toward pleasurable stimuli produces more lasting change than moving away from painful stimuli. So, while berating myself for not studying enough and getting a C on the chemistry test might motivate me to study more, the reward of getting an A on a test will be much more motivating than berating could ever be. It will also have the added benefit of prompting me to study more on a consistent basis in numerous classes.

Punishment only produces short-term change in our lives. If punishment happens too often or is too severe, it causes us to shut down and stop trying at all. The problem with calling myself a worthless idiot when I make mistakes is that, eventually, I stop trying to prove this wrong. At some point I will accept myself as a worthless idiot who can't make good decisions and begin living this out. Similarly, the problem with berating our children when they make mistakes is that they gradually grow to believe they are never going to get it right. They conclude they are just bad and wrong and quit trying to do anything differently.

How Is Judgment Harmful?

All-or-Nothing Thinking

When we think in terms of good and bad, right and wrong, should and shouldn't, beautiful and ugly, and so on, we become very black-and-white in our thinking. We are either good or we are bad, and there is no middle ground. When this is the case, an individual sees themselves as good only if they don't make any mistakes or do anything upsetting to others. Inevitably, they make a mistake and, when this occurs, they kick themselves out of the good category and feel they are bad. In order to stay in the good category, the individual must be constantly vigilant to avoid anything that might cause them to make a mistake or upset others. When we are stuck in such all-or-nothing thinking, we tend to see all our errors (and often the errors of others as well) as larger than life. When your spouse disagrees about how to load the dishwasher, for example, you are *right* and they are *wrong*, and there is no way to resolve the problem because someone must be right and only one of you can be right. Living in an all-good or all-bad world is incredibly anxiety provoking and makes it difficult to grow and learn new things. We very rarely do something new perfectly the first time!

Mental Filtering

Judging there is always one right and one wrong way to do things affects the lens with which we view ourselves and the world around us. If I have decided the right way to load the dishwasher is to put all the silverware in with the handle down, I am now going to filter out any facts or opinions that don't support this belief. It won't matter how much evidence there might be that my judgment was inaccurate. I have turned my opinion into a fact, and that fact is not open for revision.

While this may seem ludicrous when applied to something like loading the dishwasher, what if the opinion I have turned into a fact is that I am worthless? I believed this opinion to be a fact for years. I'm not sure exactly when it started, but it was firmly entrenched in my black-and-white mind by the time I was in middle school. Funny part is, there was more evidence I was valued by others than there was that I was worthless. While others had no doubt I contributed to the world around me in important ways, I could tell you everything a valuable person would be able to do that I couldn't do. Even when I was told my contributions were valuable and people enjoyed having me as a part of their lives, this did nothing to dissuade my judgment that I was worthless and unnecessary. I would look at things like my performance evaluations at work and say to myself, *It's only because they aren't around me all of the time and don't see all of my mistakes. If they had seen me yesterday when I had to fix my huge blunder, they would fire me.* Thus, my "I'm worthless" judgment remained an unchallengeable truth even when I was commended and given promotions.

Individuals struggling with anxiety often have a lot of mental filtering connected to bad things happening. Their fear-based judgment is that bad things always happen to them. No matter how many good things happen, they continue to hold firm to the judgment that bad *always* happens. Eventually, something does go wrong and, even though there were way more good things than bad things, their judgment that bad things always happen to them continues to reign.

Mind Reading

Moving into the position of judging my behavior and the behavior of others requires me to ascribe motive to my behavior and to the behavior of others. When I'm judging others, I begin to believe I know what they are thinking and why they are doing what they are doing. When my GPS malfunctioned, I was sure the woman who had arranged the presentation was mad at me and everyone attending the event saw me as incompetent because I was late. I had no evidence to base this judgment upon other than my own internal fear this might be what they would think.

I took my fear and turned it into a fact about them. I began to jump to conclusions based upon assumptions I made about people I didn't even know.

We often personalize the behavior of others to be statements about our worth and value. If I'm judging and my spouse is late or forgets to call, it might be because they are tied up in traffic or addressing an urgent situation, but I am likely to assume it is because they don't care about me, don't see me as worth the time it takes to call, or don't really want to spend time with me. Think about the last serious disagreement you had with someone you care about and evaluate whether part of what made this disagreement so intense was you personalizing their behavior to mean something about your worth and value. If this is what happened, you were mind reading and judging the thoughts, feelings, and behaviors of the other individual.

Tyranny of the Should/Must/Ought

People shouldn't drive slow in the fast lane . . . life should be fair . . . people should care as much about this project as I do . . . I shouldn't make mistakes . . . I shouldn't have such a hard time doing this . . . I have to be on time . . . I ought to save money . . . The list of things I should do, shouldn't do, must do, ought to do, and have to do is infinitely long and enslaving. Just composing the list above was a bit anxiety provoking! Attempting to live fulfilling this list perfectly every day is living like a hamster on one of those wheels—you run faster and faster and still can never get anywhere. No matter how much you do or how hard you try, there is always another *should*, *must*, or *ought* to take the place of the one you just accomplished. All the running keeps you from relaxing and enjoying the moment you are currently in because you are always looking at the next *should* or attempting to make sure whatever *shouldn't* happen is avoided.

How Do We Stop?

If reading the last several pages has convinced you judgment is feeding your worry and anxiety, the next logical question is, "So, how do I stop?" Judgment is a habit and, like any habit, won't automatically go away unless you deliberately learn to do something different. If I want to stop my habit of biting my lip, the first step would be to become aware of when I bite my lip. The same is true of judgment. The first step is to become aware of the judgments we are making. This sounds like it ought to be easy, but in reality it can be quite challenging. When we turn our judgments into facts, they don't feel like they are wrong. My judgment that I was worthless felt like a totally logical and realistic fact backed up by decades of data. Letting go of this judgment required me to slow down my thought processes and watch for every time I told myself *You are so worthless.* Once I identified my judgment, the next step was to look for "just the facts." The process went something like this for me:

1. "Worthless" is not a fact; it is an opinion and means different things to different people.

2. I have consistently gotten feedback throughout my life saying I am valued and the things I do are valued.

3. I work hard both at my job and outside of it to help others and do things well.

4. Everyone, no matter what their worth, makes mistakes. Making mistakes doesn't make someone worthless.

5. I know how to use a GPS, and it wasn't inappropriate for me to trust it was giving me the data I needed about when to turn.

6. Missing a turn and being late is not a sign of being less valuable or worthless.

Having identified the facts, I must also be willing to suspend, or let go of, my judgment in favor of holding on to these facts. Suspending judgment means letting go of judging something as bad, and it also means letting go of judging something as good. Suspend all judgment in favor of deciding what the most effective thing to do is, given the facts. This process is incredibly painful and difficult in the beginning, just like lifting weights is when you have never worked out before. In both cases, you must learn to use a set of muscles that haven't been used much and will need a lot of practice to be strengthened so they can consistently perform the new task. Since it is always easier to let go of judgments that aren't personally connected to us, I have listed two examples below for you to try out identifying the judgments, letting go of the judgments, and holding on to the facts instead.

Practice Example 1

Susan dresses for work, and as she gazes at her 280-pound body in the mirror, she tells herself once again, *You are so fat and ugly! No one is ever going to want to marry you.*

1. What are the judgments?
2. What are the facts?
3. What could Susan say to herself based on fact and not judgment?

"Fat" is not a fact but rather a value judgment highly dependent upon the culture you live in. Believing someone who weighs more is not desirable and will not be chosen for marriage simply because of their weight is also a judgment. The facts from this scenario are: Susan weighs 280 pounds and Susan is not currently married. It also appears to be a fact that Susan would like to be married, although this is not directly stated. Based upon these facts, Susan could tell herself she weighs more than she would like to or she weighs 280 pounds. Both of those things would be facts. She could also remind herself she can't make someone choose to marry her, but this doesn't mean she shouldn't want to be married. As she stands looking in the mirror, saying to herself, *I weigh 280 pounds and I would prefer to weigh less than this, so I'm going to need to decide what I want to do about this*, would position her to problem solve and make good decisions rather than feeling like she is a bad person and her situation is hopeless.

Practice Example 2

Tom arrives at work to discover his coworker has received the promotion he had hoped to receive. As Tom sits at his desk seething in anger, he tells himself, *My boss takes my hard work for granted. He doesn't appreciate anything I do. I'm never going to get any breaks from him because I'm not one of his favorite few.*

1. What are the judgments?
2. What are the facts?
3. What could Tom say to himself based on fact and not judgment?

In this situation, the facts include Tom wanting a promotion, Tom's coworker getting a promotion, and Tom not getting a promotion. It might be tempting to say "Tom works hard" is a fact, but that is actually Tom's opinion about his work. We don't know what the facts are about how hard Tom does or doesn't work. Tom's judgment is he works hard, his boss takes his work for granted, his boss does not see him as one of his favorites, and Tom is never going to get "a break." If Tom returns to his desk after learning of his coworker's promotion and says to himself, *I really wanted the promotion, and I'm disappointed I didn't get it.*

I feel like I work hard, and I thought I was ready for the promotion. My boss says my coworker is ready for the promotion, so I wonder if my opinion about my work is different from my boss's opinion, he would be poised to go and have a conversation with his boss to obtain more information and make a plan based upon the new information.

What Do We Do Instead?

Separating facts from feelings can help us to suspend judgment, but . . . what then? Often the facts or the feelings aren't what we wish they were or believe they ought to be. This can be distressing! Once we identify the facts, we still need to make decisions about what to do next. Dealing with situations or feelings we don't like and making healthy decisions can be easier when we suspend judgment—and if we are willing to learn and practice some new skills to replace our previous judgments.

Unconditional Acceptance

Often, what creates our intense anxiety and distress is judging what is actually occurring against what we believe "should" be occurring. Doing this often results in saying things like "This isn't fair," or "This shouldn't be happening," or "I can't stand this." At the beginning of the chapter, I talked about my GPS malfunction. When this occurred, my brain screamed, *My GPS shouldn't have disconnected. I can't be late for a presentation. I should have noticed something was wrong.* The events that occurred were not the events I believed should have occurred. The more I rehearsed all the reasons why they should not have occurred, the angrier and more anxious I became. The only way out of my distress was to unconditionally accept the events as they were actually occurring. No matter what I believed "should" have happened, the reality was my GPS did disconnect, I was late for the presentation, and I didn't notice anything was wrong initially. Until I accepted those facts and let go of what "should" have happened, I was filled with intense distress and unable to effectively make a plan to move forward.

Accepting the facts didn't mean I liked them or agreed with them, it meant I was willing to embrace them as reality and let go of believing reality should be different. Accepting my GPS had malfunctioned and I was going to be fifteen minutes late allowed me to make a plan for how to deal with the situation and move forward. Unconditionally accepting things exactly as they are is difficult when the situation is painful. We don't want to experience pain, disappointment, or loss, and we believe if we push these emotions away hard enough, we can avoid them. Attempting to do this is like attempting to hold a beach ball under water—it takes a lot of energy to keep it submerged, and inevitably it will find a way to pop to the surface with more energy than it had when you pushed it under the water. Attempting to avoid painful experiences or emotions causes the thoughts and feelings connected to them to intensify and, thus, be more difficult to manage.

Unconditionally accepting reality means letting go of your internal dialogue about how wrong, unfair, or unmanageable the situation is in favor of accepting thoughts like, *This is the situation I'm in, and God is in it with me. Accepting this doesn't mean I approve of it or think it is okay, but it does mean I'm going to figure out how to deal with it rather than continuing to focus on my belief it shouldn't have happened.* If you're like me, you read those last lines and thought, *Yeah, right.* Unconditionally accepting reality isn't easy. It takes a lot of practice every day with small things. Driving, shopping, and dealing with coworkers all provide wonderful opportunities to practice. Next time you are caught in road construction, instead of berating the construction crew and all the slow drivers in your head, practice accepting, *Traffic is moving very slowly right now. It isn't good or bad, it is what is currently happening because the road crew is working on this stretch of road right now.* Work to accept this fact and decide how you are going to handle the spare time in the car rather than continuing the tirade in your head about how stupid and unacceptable it is. You can do this same thing when standing in a crowded grocery store checkout or when dealing with a coworker's annoying habit.

Unconditionally accepting reality doesn't mean you won't feel pain, disappointment, or sadness. It does mean you won't intensify this emotion and make the situation or your feelings worse. If your spouse leaves your marriage, you will feel sadness, rejection, and loss. However, telling yourself, *This shouldn't be happening* and *I can't stand living without him/her* will make your emotions more intense and difficult to manage and will also make it difficult for you to effectively construct a plan to move forward with your life. Unconditionally accepting that your spouse made a decision you don't like but you need to deal with effectively allows you to begin to heal and move forward with your life.

By practicing unconditional acceptance in everyday situations, you build your capacity to utilize this skill effectively. Having developed the habit will also make it easier to draw on this skill in more painful and anxiety provoking situations such as death or divorce.

Do What Brings Life

Back in the garden of Eden there were two special trees—the tree of the knowledge of good and evil (judgment) and the tree of life. We were created to feast upon things that bring life: life to us as individuals, life to our families, and life to the world around us. Instead of fixating on making the "right" decisions, we can provoke much less anxiety by focusing on what will bring life in the situation. If something is life-giving, it causes us to grow spiritually, emotionally, mentally, or physically toward becoming everything

counter, or leaving the house in the morning with my bed unmade. Those are my opinions (preferences), and there is absolutely nothing wrong with them . . . as long as I don't make them into facts. When I go from stating "I prefer to wear blouses that come up to my collarbone" to telling myself or others that wearing low-cut blouses is wrong or immoral, I morph my opinion into a fact and then judge myself and others based upon this new "fact." When we get into the habit of making our opinions into facts, we create additional anxiety for ourselves and everyone around us. Owning my preference for wearing blouses that fit my body in a certain way frees me to dress in ways I find comfortable while allowing others the freedom to decide what is best for them. Unless they ask for my opinion about how they are dressing, I don't really need to form an opinion about their choices. It is important to form opinions about your life and the things that matter to you while refraining from feeling the need to have opinions about others or things that have nothing to do with you.

Building This Skill

Below are five activities you can use to practice building this skill. By planning each of these five activities into your week and repeating them weekly, over time they will become a natural part of your life. As this happens, you will be able to access the skills even when you are in stressful and anxiety provoking situations. Start by doing them in situations that are not anxiety provoking so you have the mental and emotional energy necessary to learn something new.

1. **Identify two common words you use today to judge yourself.** Examples might be: "I was so stupid when I . . ." or "I can't believe I was so lazy I didn't . . ." Once you have identified the words you use, work to change your

judgment into a statement of feeling. Examples of how to do this using the statements from above might include, "When I dropped the glass on the floor in the cafeteria at work, I felt stupid," or "When I realized I watched Netflix for two hours and didn't fold the laundry or empty the dishwasher, I felt like I had been lazy." Notice the difference between the emotional impact of telling yourself you *are* your feelings and simply verbalizing that you feel *something*. See if you can consistently state what you feel instead of judging yourself to be your feeling.

2. **Count your judgments.** One way to reduce unwanted behavior is simply to count the times you engage in the behavior. By making yourself more aware of when you are doing something, you automatically begin to stop doing it as much. So, take a set period of time each day (somewhere between ten minutes and eight hours, depending on how much you tend to judge and how much mental energy you must give to this task) and count your judgments during that period. Keep a tally of them on a sticky note or index card. Don't judge yourself for judging and don't attempt to change the judgment; just notice you judged, make a tally mark, and move on.

3. **After you have gotten ready for your day, look in the mirror and practice nonjudgmentally naming the facts about what you see.** Refuse to judge those facts as good or bad. Work to accept what you see without judgment and without forming opinions.

4. **Commit to turning one situation that doesn't go the way you expect today into an opportunity to practice unconditional acceptance.** Instead of ruminating about what "should" be happening, work to embrace the situation just as it is without judging it as good or bad. If you are

able, move from unconditionally accepting the situation to identifying one thing you can do to be effective in the situation.

5. **Pick one situation today and practice looking for what you can do to be effective and bring life to you and others around you.** Remember it must be effective and life-giving in both the short and long term.

CHAPTER TEN

COMPETENT FOR LIFE?

A s we begin this chapter, I would like you to ask yourself two questions:

1. Am I a competent and capable adult?
2. Do I believe God is trustworthy?

Most Christians, if polled, would answer yes to both. This answer represents our stated beliefs—the things we cognitively believe to be true. What we believe plays a huge role in how we perceive the world around us, interpret events, and choose our responses to those events.[1] For example, if I believe the world to be flat, it will affect what I believe to be true when a boat disappears over the horizon, how large I believe the world to be, and what choices I am willing to make about sailing.

Stated versus Enacted Beliefs

We have stated beliefs about many things—how money should be spent, how we should treat our spouse and children, whether we should lie, how we should treat our body, and the list goes on. In chapter 4 we talked about factual, pattern, and episodic memories. Stated beliefs are highly informed by our factual memory—the things we have been taught are facts and, therefore, are trustworthy and true. I will continue to believe the world is flat until someone I view as reputable is able to utilize data I consider to be reliable to convince me it is round. At that point, my stated value will change and I will unequivocally believe the world is round. At least that is what I will tell you I believe.

In addition to stated beliefs, we also have enacted beliefs—beliefs we act upon. While I might have changed my factual understanding and now believe the world is round, experientially I have acted upon the belief that the world is flat for years. Changing my enacted beliefs will require me to behave in different ways. To enact this belief, I will need to put my stated belief into practice, step into a boat, sail toward the place where I have witnessed other boats dropping out of sight, and determine if they have indeed fallen off the edge of the earth. Similarly, while many of us would say we believe lying is wrong, when asked by someone we care about if the dress they are wearing makes them look fat, our enacted belief might prove to be we will lie if we believe the truth will unnecessarily hurt their feelings. Our enacted beliefs are based upon our interpretation of the experiences we have had in our life, making enacted beliefs more emotionally powerful than stated beliefs.

Mindset

Going back to the questions I posed at the beginning of the chapter: most of us factually believe we are competent adults and God is trustworthy. We have been told this is true by teachers, pastors, and other trusted individuals; we can quote Scriptures we were taught as children saying it is true; and we have accomplishments like graduating from high school to support the veracity of these beliefs. However, we also have a plethora of experiences that may have caused us to experientially conclude something different. We all enter the world as infants: incompetent to care for ourselves and incapable of surviving in the world without others to do things for us we cannot do for ourselves. Regardless of how wonderful our childhood may have been, everyone's childhood experientially consisted of wanting to do something we were incapable of doing, failing to do it repeatedly, and, after repeated failure, sometimes learning to do it proficiently. This process of learning is normal, and the things we experienced while learning formed our beliefs about ourselves and our competency. If a three-year-old learning to button their shirt has parents who repeatedly become frustrated with the child's clumsy attempts to make their fingers work right, pushes them out of the way while commenting either verbally or nonverbally, "What in the world is wrong with you that you are too stupid to know how to do something as simple as this?" and proceeds to button the shirt for them, the child learns to experientially believe:

- I am stupid.
- I shouldn't need to practice in order to learn things. If I do, there is something wrong with me.
- I can't do things for myself and need others in my life to do things for me.

On the other hand, if a child's feeble, three-year-old attempts to button their shirt are met by parents who encourage them with, "This is hard to learn and you are doing great. Take a deep breath and try again!" while they patiently coach the child until they learn to do it themselves, the experiential beliefs the child develops might include:

- Learning is hard work and requires repetition, but I can do it.

- When something is hard, step back, take a breath, and try again.
- My experience is similar to what others experience.

While both children will likely grow up to state they are competent adults, if they each had pervasive experiences like those experienced in learning to button their shirt, their enacted beliefs would likely look quite different. Their stated beliefs are what they want the world to believe. Their enacted beliefs are what they internally experience as reality and determine how they interpret the events of their life. Our enacted beliefs form our mindset—the established set of beliefs we hold about ourselves and the world around us.

Our mindset determines how we interact in the world as well as what data we attend to and what data we exclude within our world. If we were to be aware of and attempt to make meaning of each of the eleven million pieces of information entering our brains through our senses every second,[2] it would literally overwhelm us and likely create an inability to function. Instead, we selectively attend to a small portion of this data and exclude the rest. This process of selective attention allows us to exclude data that doesn't support our stated or enacted beliefs while attending to the data that lines up with what we believe to be true about ourselves and the world around us.

For example, my nickname while growing up was "Stupid." Every mistake I made became evidence this label was right and I was, in fact, stupid. Taking standardized tests where I performed well above average did nothing to dissuade me of this belief. Even getting straight As throughout graduate school didn't disprove my enacted belief I was stupid. I selectively attended to all my mistakes and excused or excluded all data supporting my intelligence. When I got an A on a test, my explanation was literally, "I just happened to study the right material. If the professor had chosen different questions, I would have failed." This explanation allowed my enacted belief and mindset about my intelligence to remain unchallenged in the face of data refuting it. The discrepancy between my stated belief that I was of average intelligence and my enacted belief that I was, in actuality, stupid created a great deal of anxiety as well as a need to ensure no one discovered my "stupidity." I desperately wanted my stated belief to be what was true. I was terrified of others discovering the truth that I was stupid. This meant I spent every waking moment attempting to make sure I didn't make mistakes or do/say anything that would expose my lack of intelligence. The only way to do this was to avoid challenging new activities I wasn't sure I already knew how to do and make sure I was always meeting the expectations of those around me. I developed what Dr. Carol Dweck refers to as a fixed mindset.[3]

Fixed Mindset

Within a fixed mindset, an individual believes the capability or intelligence they have at this moment represents their maximum capability. Because they are innately aware of the places in their lives where their current capabilities are lacking but don't believe these are changeable, they compensate by attempting to *appear* competent and capable at all times. This preoccupation with making sure others see them as competent instead of becoming aware of their incompetence causes them to avoid challenges, give up easily when faced with obstacles, believe expending effort to learn and grow won't produce positive results, and ignore or be deeply wounded by constructive criticism that could help them to grow.[4]

Individuals with a fixed mindset frequently have an enacted belief that they are not competent to face the challenges of this world. This belief creates incredible anxiety. To deal with this anxiety and maintain their façade of being competent, they spend their lives attempting to determine all the things that might happen ahead of time so they can have a plan in place to handle these things if they do happen. Using the Boy Scout motto of "always be prepared" as their justification, their internal dialogue is comprised of anxious "what if" questions. A parent's teenager is ten minutes late for curfew and the parent's mind goes to, *What if they are at a party drinking? What if they got picked up for drunk driving, or worse, what if they were in a car accident? What if they are dying right now and I'm sitting here on my couch? What if I shouldn't have let them go and they are dead now because of my bad decision?* The list of "what if" questions goes on infinitely. Not only do they ask all these questions in their head but they also attempt to figure out how they would handle each of these situations to be "prepared" in case it does happen. While this can seem like wisdom, it doesn't actually work any better than hitting your finger repeatedly with a hammer in case you happen to slam it in the door later in the day.

When we become fixated on creating solutions for all the possible scenarios of things that could go wrong, it leaves us ill-equipped to handle whatever does happen. I sometimes use this picture in therapy to help my clients understand: I am a positively awful tennis player (fact, not opinion!) who has a very limited ability to hit the ball with my forehand, no ability to hit the ball with my backhand, and probably a 1 in 30 chance of being able to serve the ball without faulting. My son played on the high school tennis team and frequently wanted me to help him practice. To compensate for my weakness as a player, I would attempt to predict where he might hit the ball and get there before he had hit it in hopes of positioning myself to use my forehand and increase my odds of hitting the ball. This, inevitably, left me out of position for where he actually hit the ball. I had attempted to predict the "what if" and develop a strategy to deal with it. When reality didn't match my "what if" (which occurred most of the time), the energy I had expended attempting to create a solution for my "what if" left me ill-prepared to handle real life. The same is true when we spend our lives attempting to handle all the "what ifs" ahead of time. It takes a ton of time and energy to run all the "what if" scenarios in our head and create solutions. The time we spend creating solutions is time we are distracted from what is actually happening around us. The energy we expend also depletes our resources for dealing with what actually occurs. At best, all the "what ifs" create an ongoing pattern of worry and, at worst, feed anxiety disorders.

Is God Trustworthy?

Our enacted belief that we are not competent and capable affects our mindset toward the world around us. Our enacted beliefs around the question of God's trustworthiness are equally important in determining our view of ourselves as capable to successfully handle our lives. Children are not competent and capable of handling life without the consistent assistance of caring adults. Additionally, children do not have the reasoning capabilities of adults. A child's brain thinks in black-and-white absolutes and is egocentric, meaning their ability to see things from another's point of view is extremely limited. This explains how a child explodes, "I hate you!" when told by their father they can't have the new toy they just spied on the shelf at Walmart. Most of us, if we are honest, can still have difficulty seeing things from another's point of view and identifying and accepting that there are gray areas instead of operating out of a black-and-white mindset. It is difficult to see your spouse as loving you well when they are unwilling to do things the way you believe they should be done. We struggle to step into their shoes, see the world from their point of view, and avoid thinking about them as wrong while we are right. It is easier to trust your spouse and believe they are on your team and will be by your side when they are doing the things you want them to do. It is more difficult to believe these same things when they are not doing the things you want them to do—even if these things are actually in your best interest.

Our ability to trust God is similar to our ability to trust others. God seems perfectly trustworthy when he answers our prayers for safety, the salvation of those we love, protection from life-threatening illnesses, and a comfortable, financially secure life with people we enjoy being with. We view God as trustworthy when he provides us with a safe and secure life filled with the people, things, and experiences we want. Unfortunately, this isn't the life God promised to provide and frequently isn't the life that is in our best interest. However, we aren't much different from the little kid who wants the new toy from Walmart. When we don't get what we want, we have difficulty seeing how this could be good and how it is possible for a God who didn't provide what we wanted to be loving. We are not alone in this struggle. Scripture is replete with examples of the Israelites concluding God was not trustworthy or good because things were not going the way the people believed they should—in fact, they were willing to have Jesus crucified because he wasn't being a savior who overthrew the Roman government and established himself as king.

God parted the Red Sea so the Israelites could walk across on dry land and then killed all the Egyptians chasing them (Exod. 14:21–29). The Israelites responded by singing, "The LORD is my strength and my defense; he has become my salvation. . . . In your unfailing love you will lead the people you have redeemed. In your strength you will guide them to your holy dwelling" (15:2, 13). A mere three days later, when they couldn't find water to drink, they complained it would have been better if God had left them in Egypt. They had seen God control water by parting the Red Sea and yet they didn't believe he would continue to provide for them because it wasn't happening in their timeframe and the way they wanted it to. God not only provided water but also went on to provide them with manna when they didn't have anything to eat. His instructions for the manna were, "The people are to go out each day and gather enough for that day" (16:4). He had already proven his capacity to rescue them from their enemy and provide water when they needed it. His promise to provide what was needed each day should have been trustworthy . . . right? Yet some of the Israelites found themselves fearing, *What if God doesn't give us more tomorrow?* and attempted to gather more than one day's worth. The extra rotted, and the time they spent collecting it was wasted.

While we factually know God to be trustworthy, we often have experiences where he hasn't provided what we wanted him to provide, when we wanted him to provide it, in the way we wanted him to provide it. He didn't give the Israelites a detailed plan for how they would get to the promised land . . . he didn't tell the Jews how he would establish his kingdom here on earth . . . and he doesn't tell us how he will get us through the hardships we face.

Just like we selectively attend to data that supports our enacted beliefs and mindset about ourselves, we selectively attend to data that supports our enacted beliefs and fears about God. The Israelites disregarded all the data about God's faithfulness when things didn't go the way they expected them to in favor of focusing on what was "wrong." We do the same thing. This leaves us with a stated belief that God is trustworthy and memorized Scripture verses to back this up—while we live out of the enacted belief that our lives should look a certain way. Since God can't be trusted to do what we believe he should, we decide we must take care of ourselves.

Sometimes the experiences that created this mindset are huge and unexplainable experiences. For example, if God is capable of healing, how can he allow a newborn child to die after the parents have implored him to heal their child? Our finite minds cannot conceive of a way this can be loving, and we struggle to live with things we don't understand and can't explain. Concluding God is not trustworthy and won't come through for us explains the events and gives us a strategy for making sure more bad things don't happen—we will just take care of ourselves.

Results of Enacted Beliefs

Our internal view of ourselves as less than competent, combined with our view of God as not trustworthy, leaves us in a precarious situation. We were created to live interdependent lives, intimately connected to God and others. Our fear of being discovered as a fraud who is incompetent or less competent than those around us causes us to distance ourselves from others and project an image of competence even when we are feeling deeply afraid and incompetent. Our fear God won't meet our needs or won't do so in the ways we believe he should causes us to be self-reliant, attempt to pull ourselves up by our bootstraps, predict all of the things that might go wrong, and ensure we have a plan and the resources to deal with all possible outcomes at all times. Talk about anxiety producing! Fortunately, we don't have to stay in this place. If we are willing to risk challenging our mindset and enacted beliefs, we can begin to operate from a growth mindset instead of a fixed mindset. We can then learn to rely upon God to be with us and provide what we need in every situation—even if it isn't what we want.

Redefining Competence

My experience taught me that, because I didn't know all the answers and made mistakes, I was stupid. I then began focusing exclusively on the things I didn't know or did wrong and discounted all other data. My journey to believing something different about myself required redefining what it meant to be competent. Defining competence as possessing all the answers and knowing how to do all things right left me (and everyone else) in the position of being incompetent and needing to hide this fact. Competence, appropriately defined, is the ability and knowledge to do something successfully. Nowhere in this definition does it say we aren't going to need to learn or have the help of others.

Competence isn't knowing all the answers but knowing how to access the resources needed to successfully accomplish something. So, I am competent to own a car, not because I know everything about how to fix the engine but because I know how to find a reputable mechanic, read the manual and determine when the car needs to be serviced, and call the mechanic when it is making noises. Having these skills allows me to competently care for an automobile even though I don't personally possess the skills to fix every problem my car might have. I have also grown in my competence to own a car in the thirty years I have been a car owner. In the beginning, I knew how to change the tires, fill it with gas, and check the oil but didn't have much skill beyond this. If the tires needed to be rotated, a headlight needed replacing, or the battery needed to be changed, I called people I trusted who taught me how to do these things. Over time, this expanded my competence as a car owner to the point that I am now occasionally the one my children call when they have a car question. I still don't know all the answers, but I know more answers than I did when I purchased my first car.

Growth Mindset

Competence built upon learning and growing as well as knowing how to access information and assistance rather than needing to possess it all personally is an integral part of a growth mindset. Unlike a fixed mindset, a growth mindset starts from the assumption that our capacity, knowledge, and intellect are things that grow and develop over time, so we can always gain in each area.[5] If I have a growth mindset and I run into an obstacle or fail at something, it becomes a chance to learn from my mistakes and to seize an opportunity to take on a new challenge. When I experience setbacks or encounter obstacles, these become opportunities to problem solve and strengthen my ability to persevere. I'm willing to persevere because I see putting forth effort and needing to learn as a natural and normal part of everyday life. I seek out constructive criticism and view finding ways to master something I haven't yet been able to do as a healthy part of being an adult. As a competent adult, I believe I will encounter difficulties and, when I do, I will figure out how to use the resources at my disposal to appropriately deal with them.[6]

Going back to my tennis illustration from earlier in the chapter, professional tennis players see themselves as competent and work from a growth mindset. A professional tennis player positions themselves in the middle of the court with their weight equally distributed so they are ready to move in any direction. They don't start to move until the ball is hit. Sometimes they choose to move and return the ball and sometimes they judge the ball is going to be out of bounds or in a position impossible to appropriately get to, so they stay exactly where they are. They know the resources they have available and they draw upon these resources to play each shot to the best of their ability. They aren't rehearsing what they "should" have done on the previous shot while playing the current shot. They also aren't standing on the baseline contemplating and attempting to prepare for all the "what if" scenarios. Their attention is 100 percent on the present moment. They see themselves as equipped to deal with whatever comes across the net. Professional tennis players also have coaches—individuals they rely upon to give them advice and help them to become stronger, better players. If they struggle when their opponent hits drop shots, they will spend time identifying what isn't working and honing the skills necessary to become proficient in this skill. Instead of seeing themselves as a failure, they constantly identify areas where they can grow and work for hours on end to become better. In their world, "always be prepared" means accurately assessing their strengths and weaknesses as a player, working in practice to grow their skills, and entering each game prepared to deal with each shot as it comes across the net.

Individuals with a growth mindset approach life with this same attitude. They are aware of their strengths and weaknesses as an individual, see each day as an opportunity to learn and grow their skills, and approach life as a series of problem-solving opportunities where they can learn and grow. Instead of running "what if" scenarios and attempting to have a solution to any potential problem, individuals with a growth mindset see themselves as equipped with a set of talents and skills, the ability to creatively problem solve, and a network of people they can tap into to help them solve the problems or overcome the obstacles they encounter. A parent with a growth mindset whose teenager isn't home ten minutes after curfew would probably feel a bit anxious but wouldn't begin to run down the list of all the things that could go wrong. Instead, viewing themselves as competent to handle whatever happens, they would decide how long they were willing to wait and what they would do if their teen hadn't arrived home within that timeframe. If it turns out their teen had been involved in some sort of accident, having stayed in the present moment and viewed themselves as competent, with the help of God and others, to handle whatever happens would have positioned them with the emotional and mental energy necessary to deal with the situation as effectively as possible.

God's Ways Are Not Our Ways

God may not do what we want him to do, when we want him to do it, and how we want him to do it. However, this doesn't mean he cannot be trusted. As a young adult, I found myself angry with God for not rescuing me from a situation Scripture clearly stated he did not endorse and could prevent. As I sat in my anger and rehearsed all the ways God could have changed this situation, a subtle change began to occur . . . I moved from being angry with God to being angry with God *and* questioning his character. While this might seem like a subtle shift, it is a shift with catastrophic consequences. God is infinite, and he sees and knows things we can never see or know. It is much like a child's relationship to a parent, and God used exactly this relationship to address my growing assault on his character.

My son was eighteen months old around this time, which meant he needed his immunization shots, so I dutifully arrived at the doctor's office. This was not the first set of shots my son had received, so he was more than a bit upset at the prospect of facing this event. Following the nurse's instructions, I firmly pinned my screaming son to the table as the needle was jabbed into his leg. In the midst of this, I sensed God saying, *This is what's happening between you and me.* As I reflected upon this that evening after settling my children in bed, the parallel was driven home. From my son's vantage point, his mother—the woman who was supposed to love and protect him from everything bad in the world—was holding him down and allowing something awful to happen to him. No explanation I could give him for why I was allowing this to happen would ever make sense to him, and I didn't expect it to. *I* knew this momentary pain would prevent horrible and awful things he might not survive from happening. *He,* on the other hand, would never be able to see this and would hopefully never experience the greater pain because I was allowing him to experience this momentary pain. I was fine with him screaming and being upset about what was happening. The key: he had to be willing to allow me to scoop him up into my arms and comfort him. He had to continue to trust me to be his source of comfort and run to me instead of away from me.

The same was true between God and me. Although I have a bit more understanding today than I did as a young adult, I firmly believe I still don't fully understand what God saw that caused him to allow the painful experiences of that year into my life. From my vantage point, God stepping in and stopping the events seemed like the best and most godly solution to the problem. God didn't explain himself to me, but he was present throughout everything I was going through. When I began to shift from being angry about the circumstances to assaulting God's character, I subtly began to move him out of the position where I could run to him and allow him to be my source of comfort. When I could acknowledge to God I was angry about what was happening and angry he hadn't fixed it, and do so without changing his character, I was positioned safely within his arms where he could comfort me and be with me amid the awfulness.

God promises, "In this world you will have trouble" (John 16:33), but also promises, "The LORD himself goes before you and will be with you; he will never leave you nor forsake you. Do not be afraid; do not be discouraged" (Deut. 31:8). When we experience the "trouble" God has told us will be present in this world, we tend to ascribe responsibility for this to God and use it as evidence he has forsaken us and we are alone. Instead, he invites us to remember that this world is currently under the dictatorship of the enemy, who is seeking to "steal and kill and destroy," and Jesus has come so we can "have life, and have it to the full" (John 10:10) in the midst of the trouble we experience. He doesn't promise to remove the trouble but to be present with us and bring life in the middle of it. Jesus reminded his disciples, "Are not two sparrows sold for a penny? Yet not one of them will fall to the ground outside your Father's care. And even the very hairs of your head are all numbered" (Matt. 10:29–30). The Father doesn't promise the sparrow won't fall from the sky but does promise it won't happen without his presence.

Increasing Awareness of God's Presence

Just like my son had to choose to reach out and allow me to scoop him up into my arms, we must practice being aware of God's presence with us and his provision for us amid the circumstances in our lives. My son had to choose to risk believing I would comfort him. Choosing to trust God's promise to be with us and provide what we need requires us to risk as well. It is easy to focus on what isn't going the way we believe it should or what is causing us pain. It is much more difficult to focus on what is going right and on God's presence.

The Israelites' view of time can be helpful in learning this practice. They viewed time as circular, just like they saw nature as circular—the moon followed the sun and day followed night, cyclically. Things that had happened could be counted on to happen again. Therefore, it was important to understand what had happened in the past because it showed what could be counted on to happen in the future.[7] This is very different from the Greek and European view of time as a linear process moving toward the future and what is going to happen.[8] The Israelites looked to their past as a way of knowing what was going to happen in the future. They retold the stories of God's faithfulness and, as a result, expected to encounter this same faithfulness in their current circumstances. Whenever they took their eyes off his past faithfulness, they quickly became overwhelmed by their circumstances and began to doubt his presence with them. The same can be said in our lives. If we are willing to look for the evidence of his faithfulness daily and rehearse this, it will remind us of God's presence with us during our current circumstances—even when they are painful and difficult. We will begin to look for and expect in our current circumstances the same faithfulness and provision we have experienced in the past.

We know the story of how God provided the Israelites with manna and quail daily because the Israelites retold this story for generations when they read the Torah. In fact, part of every young Israelite boy's education was to memorize the Torah—to memorize the stories of God's faithfulness. While we would love it if God had shown them one time he was faithful and they had forever been able to act upon this newfound understanding, this wasn't the case for them and isn't the case in our lives either. The Israelites wandered in the desert for forty years, learning every day God would provide what they needed. It took forty years of seeing God provide exactly what they needed to eat, drink, and keep them safe from their enemies for them to develop an enacted belief that they could trust him. We see this enacted belief lived out when they arrive at the Jordan River for the second time and are ready to cross over into the promised land.

When they arrived at the Jordan River it was at flood stage, which meant it was 140 feet wide and at least ten feet deep because it was flowing outside its banks.[9] Not only did they need to cross this river while it was at flood stage but God also didn't tell the water to stop flowing ahead of time like he did at the Red Sea. This time, he told the Israelites they would need to step into the river before anything was going to happen (Josh. 3:8). Stepping into the river required fighting through the mire and taking the risk of stepping from the safety of the bank into murky water of uncertain depth flowing at breakneck speed. The Israelites had repeatedly recounted the stories of God parting the Red Sea and God providing clean drinking water for them out of a rock and out of bitter, undrinkable springs. Now they needed to draw upon their repeated experiences of his faithfulness and trust he would provide what they needed when they did as he asked. They had to risk trusting he would be with them when they couldn't see how this was going to work ahead of time. Their faith had been built on previous encounters of his goodness. They had to have faith the God who had taken care of them for forty years would take care of them as they stepped into the Jordan.

Like the Israelites, each of us has years of experiencing God's faithful provision of what we need. However, unlike the Israelites, most of us haven't spent years rehearsing the stories of his provision. To build an enacted belief of God's faithfulness, we will need to change this! Scripture gives us a framework for this. Paul teaches:

> Let the peace of Christ rule in your hearts, since as members of one body you were called to peace. And be thankful. Let the message of Christ dwell among you richly as you teach and admonish one another with all wisdom through psalms, hymns, and songs from the Spirit, singing to God with gratitude in your hearts. And whatever you do, whether in word or deed, do it all in the name of the Lord Jesus, giving thanks to God the Father through him. (Col. 3:15–17)

It can be easy to read this and then feel like being a good Christian means we must be thankful for all the bad things in our life, but this is not what Paul is referencing. The Israelites were not called to be grateful for the Jordan being at flood stage. They were called to stand at the edge of the Jordan and gratefully remember all the ways God had been with them and proven he would always be with them over the course of the last forty years. The same is true in our lives. Paul is asking us to take time every day to look for the ways God has been faithfully with us and taken care of us each day. Some days this can be easy to see—our spouse does something amazingly sweet, our child recovers from a serious illness, we get the job we have always wanted. Other days it can be much more difficult to see God's faithful provision because we are in the midst of horrible situations and facing great hardship. However, even in the most awful situations, God is still with us and is still taking care of us. Taking time to look for this and keeping a record of it to look back on will help us to build an enacted belief that God is trustworthy and will provide what we need during whatever we are facing. Individuals like Ann Voskamp, in her book *One Thousand Gifts*, have created practical ways for beginning to keep a record of God's faithfulness. It may be helpful to invest in a resource like this to provide structure and guidance as you begin this practice. Building an awareness of God's provision and presence and rehearsing our personal history with him is how we "put legs under" Paul's admonishment that we be thankful in everything.

I would like to tell you that my experience of God showing me how he was caring for me, just like I was caring for my son by making sure he had his immunizations, subsequently allowed me to trust God perfectly during my awful experiences. However, that is far from what happened. My experience allowed me to begin shifting my perspective so I was no longer assaulting God's character. Over the next several years, I still experienced tremendous pain and heartache. However, as I walked through those years, God faithfully gave me what I needed each day. I look back on those years now and still have no idea how I got through them. What I can tell you are stories of how God directed people to knock on my door at just the right time, faithfully provided the food I literally needed for each day, and emotionally sustained me through what felt unsurvivable most days. I have journals full of two things: stories of how God was present and pages of painful, gut-wrenching pleas for him to change my circumstances.

Scripture is full of these same things: stories of God's presence and provision intermingled with the distressing cries of his people begging him to provide what they want/need. The key is to do both. We need to look for and recount the evidence of his provision and faithfulness and also to run into his arms and allow him to comfort us in the midst of our distress. When we are able to honestly and completely share our deepest pain with him *and* faithfully believe the God who has been tangibly present with us and caring for us in the past will provide exactly what we need to get through today, we can confidently and competently live in the present moment without being overwhelmed by our fear and anxiety.

If you read the last sentence carefully, you will notice I didn't say you won't have fear or anxiety. What I did promise is our fear and anxiety won't consume us. Moment by moment, God will get us through each day by being present with us and giving us the manna we need for the moment we are in—no matter how painful the moment might be.

Building This Skill

Below are five activities you can use to practice building this skill. By planning each of these five activities into your week and repeating them weekly, over time they will become a natural part of your life. As this happens, you will be able to access the skills even when you are in stressful and anxiety provoking situations. Start by doing them in situations that are not anxiety provoking, so you have the mental and emotional energy necessary to learn something new.

1. **Embrace growth.** Until the day we stand before Jesus, we will constantly be growing and becoming who God created us to be. This journey requires us to embrace our imperfections instead of condemning ourselves for them. Pick one imperfection you are currently aware of (only one!). Take a moment to look back on your life and ask God to show you how this area of your life has grown over the years. Thank him for the ways he has been working to grow you in this area of your life and for creating you capable of learning and growing. Instead of focusing on all the ways you continue to fall short, focus on and write down one small way you can work to grow. Make sure this

is something you can work on today and is small enough
to build on what you already know without setting you
up to fail. For example, if you are currently struggling
with worrying you are not doing well enough at your job,
telling yourself you are not going to worry about this at
all today is probably too big of a step. It might be more
reasonable to set a goal of periodically taking a moment—
perhaps every time you go to the restroom—to remind
yourself you are doing your best today, and if you make
mistakes, you will learn from them and do better next
time. If you use the restroom three or four times that day,
that's three or four times you can work to tell yourself
something new and different. It won't change your mindset overnight but will gradually move you toward a growth
mindset.

2. **Before you go to bed, take time to look for at least three
   ways God took care of you today.** For me, sometimes this
   can be as simple as deliberately breathing in and out and
   reminding myself God is breathing his breath into me, and
   if he were to stop thinking about me for even a second, I
   would cease to exist. It could also be a big thing like reflecting upon the fact that God put the universe together
   so the earth could sustain human life. If the earth rotated
   even slightly closer or farther away from the sun, it could
   not sustain human life. Write down your three things for
   the day and also look back over your lists from the other
   times you have paused to do this. Thank God for the ways
   he is taking care of you—both the things you have seen
   him do and the things you may not even be aware he is
   doing.

3. **Practice vulnerability.** If we continue to project to others
   things we really don't feel to be true about ourselves, we

will continue to be anxious and fearful. Pick one way to be honest with someone about what is truly going on inside of you today. You might choose not to cover up and hide a mistake you made but acknowledge it and ask for help correcting it (without beating yourself up either out loud or in your head). You could also choose to share a fear or concern instead of pretending you are fine. Be sure to pick someone you believe can be trusted with this information and start by sharing something small so trust can be built between the two of you.

4. **Watch for places where you use words like *messed up* and *failed* today.** When you become aware of them, stop and consider what you could learn. What is one thing you could take from this experience and learn as a result? What is one thing you could work to do differently next time? Instead of seeing this mistake as a "failure," what if it is showing you what your next growth opportunity is?

5. **Pick something small you can carry with you that will remind you God is with you and is taking care of you.** Ideally this would be something you can carry in your pocket or set on your desk where you will see it frequently. Each time you see or feel this object, take a moment to remind yourself, *God is with me right now. He is more real than this object. He is taking care of me this moment, and I can trust him to take care of me for the rest of today.*

CHAPTER ELEVEN

GOING FROM HERE

A s I sat down to work on this chapter, it was New Year's Day, which seemed like a particularly poignant day to be writing about how to take the information in this book and create lasting changes in your life. I began my New Year's Day by making my normal trek to the gym. While I am usually able to walk in and pick any one of the ten treadmills to use for my workout, this morning I had to wait for one to become available. For the next few weeks, the gym will be crowded. By mid-February, however, it will be back to its normal rhythm, and I will once again have my choice of treadmills. Why will the vast majority of the resolutions made in earnest on January 1 fail by mid-February? Or why, after fifteen years of working out six days a week, do I still need to deliberately decide I will go to the gym after work before I ever leave the house in the morning because it is still easier not to go? Simply put: change is hard! However, hard doesn't mean impossible. You can make changes in your life to begin eliminating worry and anxiety. Spoiler alert: it won't happen simply by reading this book, and it won't happen simply because you have enough willpower. In fact, neither of those things, in and of themselves, have any power to produce lasting change in your life.

Why Is Change So Hard?

Early in my career, I worked on a dialysis unit with patients in kidney failure. For these patients to remain functional and healthy—even with dialysis—they needed to make significant changes to their diet and their water intake. While it was clearly explained to each of them that failing to make these dietary changes would result in toxic levels of some chemicals in their body, fluid buildup in their lungs, and potential death, most of these patients struggled to make the needed changes in their life. My experience with these dialysis patients is consistent with studies showing only 9 percent of heart bypass patients make the lifestyle changes recommended by their doctor in order to avoid potential death.[1]

As medical institutions attempt to provide better treatment and lower health-care costs, studying why this occurs has become increasingly important. What emerges is a deeper understanding of how behavior patterns form and what it takes for them to change.

Our brains are designed with what seems to be a paradox: an enormous potential to change and a predisposition to keep everything exactly as it is. Our brains function by forming what are called neural pathways. These pathways are created when the same set of neurons fire in the same sequence over and over. It's much like creating a path through a jungle. The first time through the jungle, traveling will be incredibly difficult and will take an immense amount of focus, energy, and work as you pick your way through, chop down everything standing in your way, and ward off snakes and other creatures attempting to thwart your efforts. However, if you go back down the same path the next day, it will be significantly easier. If you follow this same path every day for a month or so, it will become well-worn and will require less and less effort, concentration, and work. Eventually, taking this path will be the easiest and the preferable thing to do, even if it does not lead you exactly where you want to go.

So it is with our brains. When we learn to perform an activity like writing our name, neurons in our brain send signals (called firing) to one another that keep our eyes focused and help our hands perform the appropriate motions. Initially, this takes an immense amount of thought, concentration, and effort and will probably produce a rather illegible result. However, as we continue to practice writing our name, these neurons begin to fire more rapidly and smoothly and require less and less effort to do so. As Donald Hebb described in 1949, neurons that fire together wire themselves together.[2] This process allows our brains to efficiently and effectively complete millions of complex tasks in a day while expending only minimal energy. These behaviors are habits and routines controlled by the brain's basal ganglia—within what is sometimes referred to as the reptilian brain. This part of the brain utilizes very little energy and doesn't change easily. Whenever we do things or think in ways we have in the past, we reinforce the neural connections within our basal ganglia, making this pathway even stronger.

Simultaneously, the neurons within our brains are also continually forming new connections that change what we think, how we feel, and what we do. This process, called *neuroplasticity*, is what gives us our immense potential for change. Changing a habit or way of thinking requires building new pathways, which takes effort and focused attention. It requires us to consciously think—something that occurs primarily within the prefrontal cortex of the brain. If the structures of the reptilian brain are like a fuel-efficient car with the cruise control engaged on a freeway, the prefrontal cortex is more like an ATV attempting to navigate through the jungle; it takes more energy to function. This means the process of building new neural pathways is energy intense, requires deliberate and focused attention, is emotionally uncomfortable, and is even painful at times. While we may be able to override this discomfort on January 1, when the only thing we need to do is go and work out, it will be much more difficult to cope with this same expenditure of energy and emotional discomfort in the middle of our work week when three projects are due and everything has gone wrong. When our system becomes stressed, when we are tired, or when we are distracted, our basal ganglia kicks back in. Then we will do what we have always done—even if it is not what we want to do.

All these things are at work in every human brain. However, individuals struggling with worry or anxiety have another factor operating and complicating things even further. Our brains are designed to keep us safe, which means the brain is designed to take in immense amounts of data, compare it to everything it knows about similar situations from the past, and consider what is expected to happen in the current moment in order to detect anomalies that might signal danger. When the brain detects an anomaly from either what has happened in the past or what it expects to happen in the present, the amygdala begins draining energy away from the prefrontal cortex to mobilize our fight, flight, or freeze automatic responses. This process explains why you will gasp and jump if someone unexpectedly comes around a corner. Within individuals struggling with anxiety, this process is supercharged, making their bodies move to fight, flight, or freeze in circumstances where no current danger actually exists. Even the thought of leaving the house can send the brain into fight, flight, or freeze for someone with agoraphobia.

Reading all of this, you may wonder, *Why bother trying? I'm destined to fail anyway.* While all these factors are true, understanding them will allow you to successfully take what you have learned in this book and implement it within your life. Let's look at how you can do this.

Pleasure versus Pain

Change often feels threatening to us, and we often attempt to threaten ourselves into change. However, this works directly against our brain's desire to minimize threats and maximize pleasure. Our brain's autonomic response system is well-honed to flee from threats, and our prefrontal cortex must actively convince us to approach new possible rewards until we can experience pleasure from the new activity. Once the pleasure has been experienced, we will be highly motivated to experience it again. So, if I struggle with agoraphobia and tell myself, *Stop being such a fraidy-cat and just go get in the car and go to church like normal people do*, I am threatening myself with being abnormal if I don't engage in the activity. Additionally, my amygdala has begun draining energy from my prefrontal cortex out of fear that something bad might happen if I leave the house. The adrenaline released by this fear causes me to breathe faster, sweat, experience nausea, and shake. This is incredibly painful both physically and emotionally, so my brain is highly motivated to do whatever it takes to make these feelings stop. The only positive thing to move toward is the comfort of my living room, making this a highly enticing solution. The moment I make the decision not to leave the house, my brain will begin calming and I will feel better (more pleasure than I was feeling before), which reinforces my belief that staying at home is better than leaving. This same process is why a doctor telling a patient, "You need to lose weight, exercise more, and stop smoking or you are going to need a second bypass surgery," only works 9 percent of the time. There is a long history of pleasure involved with doing the now-forbidden activities and only emotional and physical pain involved in the process of learning new patterns.

On the flip side, if I have a strong fear of speaking in public, I am going to experience a great deal of distress as I prepare for a presentation to my company's board of directors. However, if I can successfully complete the presentation, and it goes well, I am likely to receive positive feedback from the board of directors and my manager. When this happens, my brain is going to release dopamine, which is very pleasurable, and I will be highly motivated to do things that will re-create this release of dopamine.

The neural pathways telling me to avoid speaking in public or to avoid leaving the house are well-established, much like the Mississippi River flowing toward the Gulf of Mexico. Changing the path of such a large river would be very difficult—especially if you can't stop the water while you are attempting to do it. The same is true of attempting to change where a neural pathway runs. However, building new neural pathways is much easier than changing existing neural pathways and, as you build new neural pathways, you naturally weaken the old ones.[3]

To successfully build new neural pathways, it is important to set goals for yourself and tell yourself what you are going to do instead of telling yourself what you need to stop doing. Scripture contains many more things we are supposed to do than things we are not supposed to do. When God designed our wonderfully complex brains, he designed them to be more motivated to experience pleasure—particularly the pleasure of his presence—than to avoid pain. Understanding God loves and delights in you causes you to want to move toward him, while knowing he wants you to stop sinning tends to cause you to want to hide from him or to feel defeated. Setting a goal like, "I will grow until I'm able to meet my spouse for coffee, even if I'm anxious" gives you something positive to work toward if you currently struggle to leave the house. Take a minute now to think about a positive goal you would like to work toward as a result of reading this book.

Stages of Change

Most of us assume setting a goal for ourselves means we are now ready to make the change. Sometimes this is true, and other times it is not. In attempting to figure out why some people successfully quit smoking while others did not, James Prochaska and Carlo DiClemente developed the "transtheoretical model of behavior change," which identifies five stages of change people go through as they attempt to alter a behavior or belief.[4] It can be helpful to look at each of these stages and consider if you are in it, if you have been in it, and what it might take to move through it.

Pre-Contemplative Stage

If you are in the pre-contemplative stage of change, you might be reading this book because someone else in your life has told you that you have a problem. For example, your mother might believe you worry too much and it is destroying your relationship with your children. You may not be sure you see an issue, but you want to appease her, so you read the book she gave you. Or you may have attempted to change your fear of speaking in public in the past but were unsuccessful and froze on stage in the middle of a presentation. As a result, you no longer believe this is something you can change. If you find yourself saying something like, "Sure I worry some, but it's not a big deal," you may be in the pre-contemplative stage. If this is you, don't stop reading! Instead, consider engaging in the following activities:

1. Spend some time sitting with God and reflecting upon these truths:

   He loves and delights in you right where you are and is not withholding his love based upon any of your beliefs or behaviors.

You can't do anything to change how much he loves you.

His commitment to you becoming everything you were ever created to be will not be thwarted by anything you do or don't do.

His compassion is new every morning.

He will give you everything you need to do and be everything he has called you to do and be.

2. Research anxiety and its impact upon spiritual, emotional, relational, and physical health. Take the information in this book and find out more about each category. Then do some digging to determine what treatments have been found to be effective, what makes them effective, and how people's lives are different as a result of these treatments.

3. Put yourself in the shoes of someone who loves you or with whom you spend a lot of time (a coworker, a spouse, a child, or a parent). Then write about their experiences of interacting with you when you are worried or anxious. What do they see? What do they hear? What do they experience emotionally and relationally? You may even want to check to see if your writing is accurate (if this feels like a safe thing to do). Then think through what their experience means to you.

Contemplative Stage

If you are in the contemplative stage of change, you know you have a problem, and you are thinking about attempting to change it. However, you haven't decided to do so just yet. You may know going to a counselor would be helpful in addressing your anxiety, you have checked out the counselor's availability online, but you haven't taken the step of making an appointment yet. Part of you wants to change, and part of you is unsure this is necessary and wants to stay right where you are. As you look back, you may find you have been in this stage for a long time. Oftentimes people get stuck in this stage because they want to be sure they totally understand the problem, all its causes, and all the possible solutions.[5] This desire to have all the facts prior to making a move leaves you with a sense of uncertainty around whether the cost of change will be worth the benefits. You may find yourself saying, "I know I worry a lot, but I'm not sure what I could do about it." If this is where you find yourself, consider these activities:

1. Spend some time sitting with God and reflecting upon these truths:

   He loves and delights in you right where you are and is not withholding his love based upon any of your beliefs or behaviors.

   You can't do anything to change how much he loves you.

   His commitment to you becoming everything you were ever created to be will not be thwarted by anything you do or don't do.

   His compassion is new every morning.

   He will give you everything you need to do and to be everything he has called you to do and be.

2. Take a piece of paper and divide it into four quadrants like you see below. Then take time to honestly fill in each of the quadrants without just writing in the answers you feel you "should" include. Ask yourself, *If I were to choose to address my anxiety, how would I deal with the things written in the other three quadrants? If I choose not to address my anxiety, how will I address the items in the other three quadrants?*

Benefits of Addressing My Anxiety   Costs of Addressing My Anxiety

| | |
| | |

Benefits of Not Addressing My
Anxiety   Costs of Not Addressing My Anxiety

| | |
| | |

3. Divide a piece of paper into two columns, as below, and
   spend some time writing down who you currently are in
   the first column. Then, in the second column, make a list
   of who you believe you are called by God to be. There will
   always be a discrepancy between these two, because we
   can never become everything we were created to be in this
   lifetime. However, it is important to consider how much
   anxiety is playing a role in keeping you from being who

you were called to be and in making you who you currently are. Think through what this means to you.

Who I Am	Who I Am Called to Be

Preparation Stage

Individuals in the preparation stage have decided they want to change the problem in the immediate future and are taking little steps toward change to test out what it might be like. Sometimes those little steps are successful and sometimes they fail. For example, you may have attempted to let your daughter go on a date without worrying about her and texting her multiple times while she was out. You may have been able to successfully accomplish this, or you may have made it for the first hour and then had to check in with her to be sure she was okay. You want to change and may say things like, "I wish I could just figure out how to . . ." While you want to change, you are still doing what you have always done and don't have a systematic plan to make changes. Nonetheless, you do have a desire! If you find yourself here, work to complete these activities:

1. Remind yourself—and spend some time allowing God to remind you—that:

He loves and delights in you right where you are right now.

His love for you will never change.

His commitment to you becoming everything you were ever created to be will not be thwarted by anything you do or don't do.

His compassion is new every morning.

He will give you everything you need to do and be everything he has called you to do and be.

2. Make a plan.

Go back through the previous chapters in this book and make a list of everything you believe might help you to deal with your worry and anxiety. Make sure the things on your list are very concrete and measurable. For example, "I need to begin to practice being in the present moment at least three times every day" is both positive and measurable, while "I need to stop worrying about what might happen to my kids" is negative and harder to measure.

Take your list and prioritize it, with the things that feel most attainable on the top and the things that seem the most impossible to do right now at the bottom.

3. Identify the barriers to your success. Beside each of the things you have listed, write down what you would need, but do not currently have, in order to accomplish it. This is an important step because it helps you to identify the barriers you will need to overcome in order to be successful.

4. Recruit people to be your "cheerleaders" and your "coaches." Cheerleaders don't tell you what to do or how to do it. Cheerleaders are positive encouragers who check

in on you and are willing to show up and just be there when you are struggling. Coaches, on the other hand, help you learn to do what you cannot currently do. You need someone who will help you learn how to develop new thinking and behavior patterns as you work to develop the skills needed to manage your anxiety—just like a football coach provides instruction on how to hold and throw the ball and then has you practice doing so while providing pointers. Spouses are often good cheerleaders but *should not* be coaches if you want to keep your relationship healthy.

5. With your coach, create an action plan for the first item on your list. Be specific.

What are you going to do?

How often are you going to do it?

When are you going to do it?

What will you do if something gets in your way of being successful?

How will you know you have been successful?

Action Stage

The action stage is just what it sounds like: the stage where you put your plan into action. If you have been working on the one thing you identified in the preparation stage for at least one day, you are now in the action stage. In this stage you are consciously choosing new thoughts, beliefs, and behaviors; dealing with the barriers to change; and gradually developing new skills. You may be able to say, "Yesterday I was able to be fully present with my daughter while she was taking her bath," or "I am excited to keep working toward letting go of my compulsive desire to count things." This stage is initially highly motivating but lasts for six months—yes, *six* months! This is also where people encounter obstacles and give up. To minimize your risk of giving up, be sure to:

1. Daily sit with God and reflect on the ways he has been with you amid change. Look for places where he has been strengthening and encouraging you. Reflect upon the fact that:

   He loves and delights in you, exactly where you are right now.

   His love for you will never change.

   His commitment to you becoming everything you were ever created to be will not be thwarted by anything you do or don't do.

   His compassion is new every morning.

   He will give you everything you need to do and be everything he has called you to do and be.

   He is a good Father. Just like an earthly father delights in every little step his child makes toward learning to walk, your heavenly Father is proud of every step you have taken toward this new goal. He is not scolding you when things don't go just right but doing exactly what an earthly father would do when his nine-month-old lets go of the couch and is unable to stay upright—he picks you up, dusts you off, comforts you, and encourages you to try again while he holds on to your hands with his fingers.

2. Visualization is a key element in the action plan. Most of us have absolutely no problem visualizing ourselves failing or engaging in the behavior we don't like. The same is often not true of visualizing ourselves successfully accomplishing our new goal. When we watch someone's brain

through a Functional MRI as they engage in a behavior like playing the piano and then watch their brain while they visualize themselves engaging in this same behavior, the brain behaves *almost exactly the same* in both instances. This means visualizing yourself doing something can be almost as powerful as actually doing it.[6] Musicians and athletes visualize themselves successfully completing their activities as a normal part of their training. As they do this, they are strengthening the neural pathways associated with the activity. Take your goal and visualize yourself accomplishing this goal anxiety-free. What are the physical sensations, thought patterns, and feelings associated with accomplishing this activity successfully? Make visualizing a regular part of your day, and make sure you don't allow yourself to visualize attempting but failing.

3. Remember, this is about training, not trying. In order to develop new neural pathways, you must use these new pathways over and over until the neurons fire together enough to wire together. Just like I will never learn to be an accomplished pianist by practicing sixty minutes one day and then not returning to the piano for another week, we cannot create new patterns of thinking, feeling, and behaving without engaging in deliberate practice repeatedly until the new patterns become natural parts of how we function. In the beginning it is much like learning to walk; it takes all our attention and focus, so we need to devote specific time to this. Don't let a day go by without working on these new skills and thought patterns. Develop a training plan and stick to it . . . whether or not you feel like it. If you find yourself falling back into old thinking patterns or behavioral patterns, call your coach and your cheerleader and get back on track. If you're feeling

discouraged, call your coach, your cheerleader, and anyone else who can pray for and encourage you.

4. Expect obstacles! Remember, you have engaged in the old thought and behavior pattern for a long time, so change will be challenging but not impossible. It is very easy to focus on all the ways we were unable to engage in the new behavior but much more difficult to focus on what we did well. It is important to make sure you are focusing on the good. Take time at the end of each day to reflect upon the successes and partial successes in your day. Thank God for them and for his presence in the middle of even the most difficult circumstances.

5. Don't forget rewards! Remember, we are more motivated by those dopamine-releasing positive experiences than by anything else. Make sure you are regularly rewarding both your attempts at new behaviors and your successes. You can space your rewards out more as the new pattern develops, but in the beginning you need to reward yourself frequently. If you attempt to do something differently, it is worth rewarding!

6. Don't give in to the temptation to add on another goal after successfully accomplishing your current goal one time. This is a mistake people frequently make. This is going to take time! You have a much better chance of being successful if you move slowly than if you push yourself too fast. Crash diets don't work, and neither will pushing yourself to do everything you have read in this book at once. Remember . . . six months!

7. When you have successfully mastered the first thing on your list, and both you and your coach believe the new neural pathway is well established, repeat this process with the next thing on your list. If you attempt to add

something new and it is negatively impacting your previous goal, let go of the new goal until you have firmly reestablished the previous goal and then try again.

Maintenance Stage

When you have been able to successfully maintain your change for at least six months and are committed to sustaining this new way of living, you move into the maintenance phase. If you are maintaining your house or your car, you are regularly engaging in activities that keep it in its current condition. You change the oil in the car or change the filter in the furnace. The same is true with maintaining a new thought or behavior pattern. At the beginning of the chapter, I told you I must commit to going to the gym every morning before I go to work or I will go to my couch instead of the treadmill after work. This daily commitment is how I maintain my behavior pattern. If I begin to allow myself to make excuses and not work out, soon I am back in the pattern of never working out. In order to maintain my desired behavior, I must commit to it every day. However, because it is built into my life, it doesn't take as much work once I make the commitment. The same will be true with your new pattern. When you are in the maintenance phase, it is important to:

1. Spend time with God each day reflecting on the truth that:

   He loves and delights in you, exactly where you are right now.

   His love for you will never change.

   His commitment to you becoming everything you were ever created to be will not be thwarted by anything you do or don't do.

   His compassion is new every morning.

It is because of his empowerment combined with your willingness that you have been able to live victorious yesterday. His empowerment combined with your willingness will be necessary for you to live victorious today.

2. Look for places where old behavior patterns and thought patterns are creeping back in. This is especially important if you find yourself under more stress than normal or working to do something new. If you know something stressful is coming up, plan to provide yourself with extra support.

This book will only be useful if its contents are put into practice. I hope this chapter has given you some practical action steps. Managing anxiety and living fully present in this moment are a process that won't be fully completed until the day you stand before Jesus in your perfected state. Since it will not be finished in this life, graciously examining where you are in the learning journey and then setting goals to help yourself begin moving forward is essential. Embracing the ongoing journey of learning and becoming everything God created you to be is worth the time and energy needed. I pray you experience his love and his encouragement as you journey with him.

FEELING WORDS

Anger and Resentment

Agitated	Enraged	Miffed
Angry	Furious	Resent
Annoyed	Galled	Resentful
Bitter	Had it	Seething
Bristle	Hateful	Ticked
Bugged	Impatient	Upset
Chagrined	Indignant	Uptight
Disgusted	Infuriated	Vengeful
Dismayed	Livid	Violent

Anxiety and Tension

Afraid	Bashful	Embarrassed
Alarmed	Defensive	Fearful
Anxious	Desperate	Fidgety
Apprehensive	Distrustful	Frantic
Awkward	Dread	Frightened

Hesitant	Restless	Terror-stricken
Horrified	Scared	Threatened
Intimidated	Shaken	Timid
Jittery	Shocked	Uneasy
Nervous	Shy	Unsure
Panicky	Stunned	Uptight
Paralyzed	Tense	Vulnerable
Rattled	Terrified	Worried

Caring and Loving

Accept	Devoted	Prize
Admire	Enamored	Regard
Adore	Esteem	Respect
Affectionate	Fond	Tender
Attached	Friendly	Trust
Care	Idolize	Value
Cherish	Infatuated	Warm
Close	Like	Worship
Concerned	Love	
Dear	Positive	

Competence and Strength

Able	Effective	Resolute
Adequate	Firm	Secure
Brave	Forceful	Self-reliant
Capable	Important	Sharp
Committed	Impressive	Skillful
Competent	Influential	Strong
Confident	Inspired	Successful
Convicted	Mastery	Sure
Courageous	Potent	Trusting
Daring	Powerful	Well-equipped
Determined	Ready	

Confusion and Troubled

Adrift	Disorganized	Stumped
Ambivalent	Disturbed	Torn
Baffled	Floored	Trapped
Befuddled	Flustered	Troubled
Bewildered	Frustrated	Uncertain
Bothered	Lost	Uncomfortable
Conflicted	Mixed-up	Undecided
Confounded	Overwhelmed	Uneasy
Confused	Perplexed	Unsure
Disconcerted	Puzzled	

Depression and Discouragement

Anguished	Disheartened	Lost
Awful	Dismal	Lousy
Bad	Distressed	Low
Blah	Down	Melancholy
Bleak	Downcast	Miserable
Blue	Dreadful	Pessimistic
Brokenhearted	Forlorn	Rotten
Deflated	Gloomy	Sad
Demoralized	Grieved	Sorrowful
Depressed	Grim	Tearful
Despondent	Hopeless	Terrible
Disappointed	Horrible	Unhappy
Discouraged	Kaput	Weepy

Guilt and Embarrassment

Ashamed	Embarrassed	Horrible
Branded	Exposed	Humiliated
Crummy	Faulty	In error
Degraded	Foolish	Lament
Demeaned	Goofed	Mortified
Disgraced	Guilty	Regretful

Remorseful
Responsible
Ridiculous

Rotten
Silly
Stupid

Unforgivable
Wrong

Happiness and Satisfaction

Calm
Cheerful
Content
Delighted
Ecstatic
Elated
Elevated
Enthusiastic
Euphoric
Excited
Fantastic
Fine

Fulfilled
Glad
Glowing
Good
Gratified
Great
Happy
Hopeful
Jolly
Joyful
Jubilant
Lighthearted

Marvelous
Mellow
Pleased
Satisfied
Serene
Splendid
Super
Superb
Terrific
Thrilled
Tranquil
Wonderful

Inadequacy and Helplessness

Awkward
Clumsy
Crippled
Defeated
Deficient
Emasculated
Finished
Helpless
Immobilized
Impaired
Impotent
Inadequate

Incapable
Incompetent
Incomplete
Ineffective
Inefficient
Inept
Inferior
Inhibited
Insecure
Insignificant
Lacking
Overwhelmed

Puny
Small
Stupid
Unable
Uncertain
Unfit
Unimportant
Useless
Weak
Whipped
Worthless

Loneliness

Abandoned
Alienated

Alone
Aloof

Apart
Cut off

Distant   Forsaken   Lonesome
Estranged   Isolated   Rejected
Excluded   Left out   Remote
Forlorn   Lonely   Shut out

Rejection and Offensiveness

Abused	Discarded	Overlooked
Belittled	Discounted	Pained
Betrayed	Discredited	Rejected
Cheapened	Disparaged	Ridiculed
Criticized	Exploited	Ruined
Crushed	Hurt	Scored
Debased	Impugned	Slandered
Degraded	Maligned	Slighted
Depreciated	Minimized	Tortured
Destroyed	Mistreated	Unappreciated
Devalued	Mocked	Underestimated
Devastated	Neglected	Used
Disappointed	Offended	Wounded

NOTES

Chapter 1 Worry or Anxiety?

1. Aditi Nerurkar et al., "When Physicians Counsel about Stress: Results of a National Study," *JAMA Internal Medicine* 173, no. 1 (November 2012): 76–77, https://doi:10.1001/2013.jamainternmed.480.

2. "Facts & Statistics," Anxiety and Depression Association of America, 2010–2018, https://adaa.org/about-adaa/press-room/facts-statistics.

3. "Facts & Statistics," Anxiety and Depression Association of America.

4. "Statistics about Diabetes," American Diabetes Association, last modified March 22, 2018, http://www.diabetes.org/diabetes-basics/statistics/.

5. "Statistics about Diabetes," American Diabetes Association.

6. American Psychiatric Association, *Diagnostic and Statistical Manual of Mental Disorders*, 5th ed. (Arlington, VA: American Psychiatric Association, 2013), 202–3.

7. American Psychiatric Association, *Diagnostic and Statistical Manual of Mental Disorders*, 5th ed., 197–98.

8. American Psychiatric Association, *Diagnostic and Statistical Manual of Mental Disorders*, 5th ed., 237–38.

9. American Psychiatric Association, *Diagnostic and Statistical Manual of Mental Disorders*, 5th ed., 217–18.

10. American Psychiatric Association, *Diagnostic and Statistical Manual of Mental Disorders*, 5th ed., 280–81.

11. American Psychiatric Association, *Diagnostic and Statistical Manual of Mental Disorders*, 5th ed., 271–72.

12. American Psychiatric Association, *Diagnostic and Statistical Manual of Mental Disorders*, 5th ed., 208–9.

13. American Psychiatric Association, *Diagnostic and Statistical Manual of Mental Disorders*, 5th ed., 222.

Chapter 2 What Causes Anxiety?

1. E. Bruce Goldstein, "Individual Differences in Perception," *Encyclopedia of Perception*, 1st ed. (Thousand Oaks, CA: Sage Publications, 2010), 492.

2. Elisa Neuvonen et al., "Late-life Cynical Distrust, Risk of Incident Dementia, and Mortality in a Population-Based Cohort," *Neurology* 82, no. 24 (May 2014): 2205–12, https://doi.org/10.1212/WNL.0000000000000528.

3. Hilary Tindle et al., "Optimism, Cynical Hostility, and Incident Coronary Heart Disease and Mortality in the Women's Health Initiative," *Circulation* 120, no. 8 (September 2009): 656–62, https:doi.org/10.1161/CIRCULATIONAHA.10 8.827642.

4. "Social Determinants of Health: Know What Affects Health," Centers for Disease Control and Prevention, last modified January 29, 2018, https://www.cdc .gov/socialdeterminants/index.htm.

5. W. J. Strawbridge, "Frequent Attendance at Religious Services and Mortality Over 28 Years," *American Journal of Public Health* 87, no. 6 (June 1997): 957–61.

6. Harold Koenig et al., "Attendance at Religious Services, Interleukin-6, and Other Biological Parameters of Immune Function in Older Adults," *The International Journal of Psychiatry in Medicine* 27, no. 3 (January 1997): 233–50, https://doi.org/10.2190/40NF-Q9Y2-0GG7-4WH6.

7. Kenneth Pargament et al., "Religious Coping Methods as Predictors of Psychological, Physical and Spiritual Outcomes among Medically Ill Elderly Patients: A Two-Year Longitudinal Study," *Journal of Health Psychology* 9, no. 6 (November 2004): 713–30, https://doi.org/10.1177/1359105304045366.

8. Beth Azar, "A Reason to Believe: Religion May Fill the Human Need for Finding Meaning, Sparing Us from Existential Angst While also Supporting Social Organization, Researchers Say," *Monitor on Psychology* (December 2010), https:// www.apa.org/monitor/2010/12/believe.

Chapter 3 Biology Affects Anxiety

1. Hae-Ran Na et al., "The Genetic Basis of Panic Disorder," *Journal of Korean Medical Science* 26, no. 6 (May 2011): 701–10, https://doi.org/10.3346/jkms .2011.26.6.701.

2. Lakshmi N. Ravindran and Murray B. Stein, "The Pharmacologic Treatment of Anxiety Disorders: A Review of Progress," *The Journal of Clinical Psychiatry* 71, no. 7 (July 2010): 839–54, https://doi.org/10.4088/JCP.10r06218blu.

3. Gregor Hasler et al., "Effect of Acute Psychological Stress on Prefrontal GABA Concentration Determined by Proton Magnetic Resonance Spectroscopy," *The American Journal of Psychiatry* 167, no. 10 (October 2010): 1226–31, https:// doi.org/10.1176/appi.ajp.2010.09070994.

4. Remmelt R. Shür et al., "Brain GABA Levels Across Psychiatric Disorders: A Systematic Literature Review and Meta-Analysis of (1) H-MRS Studies," *Human*

Brain Mapping 37, no. 9 (September 2016): 337–52, https://doi.org/10.1002/hbm .23244.

5. Uwe Rudolph and Frédéric Knoflach, "Beyond Classical Benzodiazepines: Novel Therapeutic Potential of GABA^A Receptor Subtypes," *Nature Reviews Drug Discovery* 10, no. 9 (July 2011): 685–97, https://doi.org/10.1038/nrd3502.

6. Michael Liebrenz et al., "High-Dose Benzodiazepine Dependence: A Qualitative Study of Patients' Perception on Cessation and Withdrawal," *Boston Medical Center Psychiatry* 15, no. 116 (May 2015): https://doi.org/10.1186/s12888-0 15-0493-y.

7. Hillary Le Roux, Margaret Gatz, and Julie Loebach Wetherell, "Age at Onset of Generalized Anxiety Disorder in Older Adults," *The American Journal of Geriatric Psychiatry* 13, no. 1 (January 2005): 23–30, https://doi.org/10.1176 /appi.ajgp.13.1.23.

8. Gillis Samuelsson et al., "Incidence and Risk Factors for Depression and Anxiety Disorders: Results from a 34-year Longitudinal Swedish Cohort Study," *Aging and Mental Health* 9, no. 6 (November 2005): 571–75, https://doi.org/10 .1080/13607860500193591.

9. Joyce T. Bromberger et al., "Does Risk for Anxiety Increase During the Menopausal Transition? Study of Women's Health Across the Nation," *Menopause: The Journal of the North American Menopause Society* 20, no. 5 (May 2014): 488–95, https://doi.org/10.1097/GME.0b013e3182730599.

10. "Anxiety Disorders," Mayo Clinic, last modified May 4, 2018, https:// www.mayoclinic.org/diseases-conditions/anxiety/symptoms-causes/syc-20350961.

11. Joshua P. Smith and Sarah W. Book, "Anxiety and Substance Use Disorders: A Review," *The Psychiatric Times* 25, no. 10 (October 2008): 19.

12. Wilson M. Compton et al., "Prevalence, Correlates, Disability, and Comorbidity of DSM-IV Drug Abuse and Dependence in the United States: Results from the National Epidemiologic Survey on Alcohol and Related Conditions," *Archives of General Psychiatry* 64, no. 5 (May 2007): 566–76, https://doi.org/10 .1001/archpsyc.64.5.566.

13. Ronald C. Kessler et al., "Lifetime Prevalence and Age-of-Onset Distributions of DSM-IV Disorders in the National Comorbidity Survey Replication," *Archives of General Psychiatry* 62, no. 6 (July 2005): 593–602, https://doi.org/10.10 01/archpsyc.62.6.593.

14. M. G. Kushner et al., "Epidemiological Perspectives on Co-Occurring Anxiety Disorder and Substance Use Disorder," in *Anxiety and Substance Use Disorders: The Vicious Cycle of Comorbidity*, ed. S. H. Stewart and P. J. Conrod (New York: Springer, 2008), 3–17.

15. Steven E. Bruce, "Influence of Psychiatric Comorbidity on Recovery and Recurrence in Generalized Anxiety Disorder, Social Phobia, and Panic Disorder: A 12-Year Prospective Study," *The American Journal of Psychiatry* 162, no. 6 (June 2005): 1179–87, https://doi.org/10.1176/appi.ajp.162.6.1179.

16. Christopher D. Hornig and Richard J. McNally, "Panic Disorder and Suicide Attempt: A Reanalysis of Data from the Epidemiologic Catchment Area Study," *The British Journal of Psychiatry* 167, no. 1 (July 1995): 76–79, https:// doi.org/10.1192/bjp.167.1.76.

17. Malcolm Bruce et al., "Anxiogenic Effects of Caffeine in Patients with Anxiety Disorders," *Archives of General Psychiatry* 49, no. 11 (November 1992): 867–69, https://doi.org/10.1001/archpsyc.1992.01820110031004.

18. Michelle Murphy and Julian G. Mercer, "Diet-Regulated Anxiety," *International Journal of Endocrinology* (2013): 1–9, https://doi.org/10.1155/2013/701967.

19. Karen M. Davison and Bonnie J. Kaplan, "Food Intake and Blood Cholesterol Levels of Community-Based Adults with Mood Disorder," *Boston Medical Center Psychiatry* 12, no. 10 (February 2012), https://doi.org/10.1186/1471-244X-12-10.

20. Janice K. Kiecolt-Glaser et al., "Omega-3 Supplementation Lowers Inflammation and Anxiety in Medical Students: A Randomized Controlled Trial," *Brain, Behavior and Immunity* 25, no. 8 (November 2011): 1725–34, https://doi.org/10.1016/j.bbi.2011.07.229.

21. Mozhgan Torabi et al., "Effects of Nano and Conventional Zinc Oxide on Anxiety-Like Behavior in Male Rats," *Indian Journal of Pharmacology* 45, no. 5 (September 2013): 508–12, https://doi.org/10.4103/0253-7613.117784; Simone B. Sartori et al., "Magnesium Deficiency Induces Anxiety and HPA Axis Dysregulation: Modulation by Therapeutic Drug Treatment," *Neuropharmacology* 62, no. 1 (January 2012): 304–12, https://doi.org/10.1016/j.neuropharm.2011.07.027.

22. Joshua J. Broman-Fulks et al., "Effects of Aerobic Exercise on Anxiety Sensitivity," *Behavior Research and Therapy* 42, no. 2 (2004): 125–36, https://doi.org/10.1016/S0005-7967(03)00103-7.

23. Mental Health First Aid USA, *8-Hour Teaching Notes* (Washington, DC: National Council for Behavioral Health, 2015), 48.

Chapter 4 How We Think and What We Think Affect Anxiety

1. David B. Chamberlain, "The Sentient Prenate: What Every Parent Should Know," *Journal of Prenatal & Perinatal Psychology & Health* 26, no. 1 (1994/2011): 37–59.

2. David Howe, "Parent-Reported Problems in 211 Adopted Children: Some Risk and Protective Factors," *Journal of Child Psychology and Psychiatry and Allied Disciplines* 38, no. 4 (1997): 401–11, https://doi.org/10.1111/j.1469-7610.1997.tb01525.x.

3. David G. Meyers and Nathan C. Dewall, *Exploring Psychology*, 10th ed. (New York: Worth, 2016), 285.

4. Meyers and Dewall, *Exploring Psychology*, 285.

5. Daniel L. Schacter, *Searching for Memory: The Brain, the Mind, and the Past* (New York: Basic Books, 1996), 17.

6. Schacter, *Searching for Memory*, 17.

7. Schacter, *Searching for Memory*, 17.

8. Scott Stuart and Michael Robertson, *Interpersonal Psychotherapy: A Clinician's Guide* (Boca Raton, FL: Taylor and Francis Group, 2012), 21–25.

9. Sara H. Konrath et al., "Changes in Adult Attachment Styles in American College Students Over Time: A Meta-Analysis," *Personality and Social Psychology Review* 18, no. 4 (2014): 326–48, https://doi.org/10.1177/1088868314530516.

10. Konrath et al., "Changes in Adult Attachment Styles."

11. Konrath et al., "Changes in Adult Attachment Styles."

12. Meyers and Dewall, *Exploring Psychology*, 143.

13. Konrath et al., "Changes in Adult Attachment Styles."

14. Amir Levine and Rachel Heller, *Attached: The New Science of Adult Attachment and How It Can Help You Find—and Keep—Love* (New York: Penguin Random House, 2010).

Chapter 5 Social Environments Affect Anxiety

1. D. A. Chavira and M. B. Stein, "Childhood Social Anxiety Disorder: From Understanding to Treatment," *Child and Adolescent Psychiatric Clinics of North America* 14, no. 4 (October 2005): 797–818, https://doi.org/10.1016/j.chc.2005.05.003.

2. "What Is Stress?" The American Institute of Stress, accessed May 16, 2019, https://www.stress.org/what-is-stress.

3. David G. Myers and Nathan DeWall, *Exploring Psychology*, 10th ed. (New York: Worth, 2016), 368–69.

4. G. E. Miller, "The U.S. Is the Most Overworked Developed Nation in the World," *20 Something Finance*, last modified January 2, 2018, https://20something finance.com/american-hours-worked-productivity-vacation.

5. Quentin Fottrell, "People Spend Most of Their Waking Hours Staring at Screens," *MarketWatch*, last modified August 4, 2018, https://www.market watch.com/story/people-are-spending-most-of-their-waking-hours-staring-at-screens-2018-08-01.

6. Jon D. Elhai et al., "Problematic Smartphone Use: A Conceptual Overview and Systematic Review of Relations with Anxiety and Depression Psychopathology," *Journal of Affective Disorders* 207 (January 2017): 251–59, https://doi.org/10.1016/j.jad.2016.08.030.

7. Stanley Rachman, "Betrayal: A Psychological Analysis," *Behavioral Research and Therapy* 48, no. 4 (April 2010): 304–11, https://doi.org/10.1016/j.brat.2009.12.002.

8. Wikipedia, s. v. "betrayal," last modified February 19, 2019, https://en.wiki pedia.org/wiki/Betrayal.

Chapter 6 Our View of God Affects Anxiety

1. David G. Myers and Nathan C. DeWall, *Exploring Psychology*, 10th ed. (New York: Worth, 2016), 306.

2. William Morris, *The American Heritage Dictionary of the English Language*, new college ed. (Boston: Houghton Mifflin, 1981), 961.

3. *Roget's 21st Century Thesaurus*, 3rd ed., s. v. "patient," ed. The Princeton Language Institute (New York: Philip Lief Group, 2013), accessed February 2019, https://www.thesaurus.com/browse/patient?s=t.

4. *Roget's 21st Century Thesaurus*, s. v. "patient."

Chapter 7 Strategies for Dealing with Worry and Anxiety

1. *Encyclopædia Britannica*, s. v. "tabula rasa," ed. Brian Duignan, last modified February 26, 2015, https://www.britannica.com/topic/tabula-rasa.

2. Bianca Acevedo et al., "The Highly Sensitive Brain: A Review of the Brain Circuits Underlying Sensory Processing Sensitivity and Seemingly Related Disorders," *Philosophical Transactions of the Royal Society of London* 373, no. 1744 (April 2018): 1–5.

3. Marsha M. Linehan, *DBT Skills Training Manual*, 2nd ed. (New York: Gilford Press, 2015).

Chapter 8 Living in the Present Moment

1. Matthew D. Lieberman et al., "Putting Feelings into Words," *Psychological Science* 18, no. 5 (May 2007): 421–28, https://doi.org/10.1111/j.1467-9280.2007.01916.x.

2. A. R. Aaron, T. W. Robbins, and R. A. Poldrack, "Inhibition and the Right Inferior Frontal Cortex," *Trends in Cognitive Science* 8, no. 6 (April 2004): 170–77, https://doi.org/10.1016/j.tics.2004.02.010.

3. Eyal Ophir, Clifford Nass, and Anthony D. Wagner, "Cognitive Control in Media Multitaskers," *Proceedings of the National Academy of Science* 106, no. 37 (September 2009): 15583–87, https://doi.org/10.1073/pnas.0903620106.

4. "Multitasking: Switching Costs," American Psychological Association, last modified March 20, 2006, https://www.apa.org/research/action/multitask.aspx.

Chapter 9 Letting Go of Judgment

1. *The American Heritage Dictionary of the English Language*, s.v. "judgment," ed. William Morris (Boston: Houghton Mifflin, 1981), 709.

2. *The American Heritage Dictionary of the English Language*, new college ed., s.v. "effective," ed. William Morris (Boston: Houghton Mifflin, 1981), 416.

Chapter 10 Competent for Life?

1. Marlene Schommer, "Effects of Beliefs about the Nature of Knowledge on Comprehension," *Journal of Educational Psychology* 82, no. 3 (September 1990): 498–504, https://doi.org/10.1037/0022-0663.82.3.498.

2. Timothy D. Wilson, *Strangers to Ourselves: Discovering the Adaptive Unconscious* (Boston: Harvard University Press, 2004), 81.

3. Carol S. Dweck, *Mindset: The New Psychology of Success* (New York: Ballantine Books, 2016), 6.

4. Dweck, *Mindset*, 24–29.

5. Dweck, *Mindset*, 6.

6. Dweck, *Mindset*, 24–29.

7. Thorleif Boman, *Hebrew Thought Compared with Greek* (New York: W. W. Norton, 1970), 133–34.

8. Boman, *Hebrew Thought Compared with Greek*, 126.

9. John A. Beck, "Why Do Joshua's Readers Keep Crossing the River?: The Narrative Geographical Shaping of Joshua 3–4," *Journal of the Evangelical Theological Society* 48, no. 4 (December 2005): 689–99.

Chapter 11 Going from Here

1. Alan Deutschman, "Change or Die," *Fast Company*, May 1, 2005, https://www.fastcompany.com/52717/change-or-die.

2. D. O. Hebb, *The Organization of Behavior: A Neuropsychological Theory* (New York: Wiley, 1949).

3. Linda Spear, "The Adolescent Brain and Age-Related Behavioral Manifestations," *Neuroscience Biobehavioral Review* 24, no. 4 (June 2000): 417–63.

4. James O. Prochaska and Carlo C. DiClemente, "Stages and Processes of Self-Change in Smoking: Toward an Integrative Model of Change," *Journal of Consulting and Clinical Psychology* 51, no. 5 (June 1983): 390–95.

5. Carlo C. DiClemente and M. M. Velasquez, "Motivational Interviewing and the Stages of Change," *Motivational Interviewing*, ed. W. R. Miller and S. Rollnick (New York: Guilford Press, 2002), 208.

6. V. K. Raganthan et al., "From Mental Power to Muscle Power—Gaining Strength by Using the Mind," *Neuropsychologia* 42, no. 7 (2004): 944–56.

BIBLIOGRAPHY

Aaron, A., T. W. Robbins, and R. A. Poldrack. "Inhibition and the Right Inferior Frontal Cortex." *Trends in Cognitive Science* 8, no. 6 (April 2004): 170–77. https://doi.org/10.1016/j.tics.2004.02.010.

Acevedo, Bianca, Elaine Aron, Sarah Pospos, and Dana Jessen. "The Functional Highly Sensitive Brain: A Review of the Brain Circuits Underlying Sensory Processing Sensitivity and Seemingly Related Disorders." *Philosophical Transactions of the Royal Society of London* 373, no. 1744 (February 2018): 1–5. https://doi.org/10.1098/rstb.2017.0161.

American Diabetes Association. "Statistics about Diabetes." Last modified March 22, 2018. http://www.diabetes.org/diabetes-basics/statistics/.

American Psychiatric Association. *Diagnostic and Statistical Manual of Mental Disorders*, 5th ed. Washington, DC: American Psychiatric Association, 2013.

American Psychological Association. "Multitasking: Switching Costs." Last modified March 20, 2006. https://www.apa.org/research/action/multitask.aspx.

Anxiety and Depression Association of America. "Facts & Statistics." Last modified 2018. https://adaa.org/about-adaa/press-room/facts-statistics.

Azar, Beth. "A Reason to Believe: Religion May Fill the Human Need for Finding Meaning, Sparing Us from Existential Angst While also Supporting Social Organization, Researchers Say." *Monitor on Psychology* (December 2010). https://www.apa.org/monitor/2010/12/believe.

Beck, John A. "Why Do Joshua's Readers Keep Crossing the River?: The Narrative Geographical Shaping of Joshua 3–4." *Journal of the Evangelical Theological Society* 48, no. 4 (December 2005): 689–99.

Boman, Thorleif. *Hebrew Thought Compared with Greek* (New York: W. W. Norton, 1970), 126–34.

Broman-Fulks, Joshua J., Mitchell E. Berman, Brian A. Rabian, and Michael J. Webster. "Effects of Aerobic Exercise on Anxiety Sensitivity." *Behavior Research and Therapy* 42, no. 2 (2004): 125–36. https://doi.org/10.1016/S0005-7967(03)00103-7.

Bromberger, Joyce T., Howard M. Kravitz, Yuefang Chang, John F. Randolph, Nancy E. Avis, Ellen B. Gold, and Karen A. Matthews. "Does Risk for Anxiety Increase during the Menopausal Transition? Study of Women's Health Across the Nation." *Menopause: The Journal of the North American Menopause Society* 20, no. 5 (May 2014): 488–95. https://doi.org/10.1097/GME.0b013e3182730599.

Bruce, Malcolm, Nigel Scott, Philip Shine, and Malcolm Lader. "Anxiogenic Effects of Caffeine in Patients with Anxiety Disorders." *Archives of General Psychiatry* 49, no. 11 (November 1992): 867–69. https://doi.org/10.1001/archpsyc.1992.01820110031004.

Bruce, Steven E., Kimberly A. Yonkers, Michael W. Otto, Jane L. Eisen, Risa B. Weisberg, Maria Pagano, M. Tracie Shea, and Martin B. Keller. "Influence of Psychiatric Comorbidity on Recovery and Recurrence in Generalized Anxiety Disorder, Social Phobia, and Panic Disorder: A 12-Year Prospective Study." *The American Journal of Psychiatry* 162, no. 6 (June 2005): 1179–87. https://doi.org/10.1176/appi.ajp.162.6.1179.

Centers for Disease Control and Prevention. "Social Determinants of Health: Know What Affects Health." Last modified January 29, 2018. https://www.cdc.gov/socialdeterminants/index.htm.

Chamberlain, David B. "The Sentient Prenate: What Every Parent Should Know." *Journal of Prenatal & Perinatal Psychology & Health* 26, no. 1 (1994/2011): 37–59.

Chavira, D. A., and M. B. Stein. "Childhood Social Anxiety Disorder: From Understanding to Treatment." *Child and Adolescent Psychiatric Clinics of North America* 14, no. 4 (October 2005): 797–818. https://doi.org/10.1016/j.chc.2005.05.003.

Compton, Wilson M., Yonette F. Thomas, Frederick S. Stinson, and Bridget F. Grant. "Prevalence, Correlates, Disability, and Comorbidity of DSM-IV Drug Abuse and Dependence in the United States: Results from the National Epidemiologic Survey on Alcohol and Related Conditions." *Archives of General Psychiatry* 64, no. 5 (May 2007): 566–76. https://doi.org/10.1001/archpsyc.64.5.566.

Davison, Karen M. and Bonnie J. Kaplan. "Food Intake and Blood Cholesterol Levels of Community-Based Adults with Mood Disorder." *Boston Medical Center Psychiatry* 12, no. 10 (February 2012). https://doi.org/10.1186/1471–244X-12–10.

Deutschman, Alan. "Change or Die." *Fast Company* (May 1, 2005). https://www.fastcompany.com/52717/change-or-die.

DiClemente, Carlo C., and M. M. Velasquez. "Motivational Interviewing and the Stages of Change." *Motivational Interviewing*. Edited by W. R. Miller and S. Rollnick. New York: Guilford Press, 2002.

Duignan, Brian. "Tabula Rasa." *The Encyclopædia Britannica*. Last modified February 26, 2015. https://www.britannica.com/topic/tabula-rasa.

Dweck, Carol S. *Mindset: The New Psychology of Success* (New York: Ballantine Books, 2016), 6–29.

Elhai, Jon D., Robert D. Dvorak, Jason C. Levine, and Brian J. Hall. "Problematic Smartphone Use: A Conceptual Overview and Systematic Review of Relations with Anxiety and Depression Psychopathology." *Journal of Affective Disorders* 207 (January 2017): 251–59. https://doi.org/10.1016/j.jad.2016.08.030.

Fottrell, Quentin. "People Spend Most of Their Waking Hours Staring at Screens." *MarketWatch*. Last modified August 4, 2018. https://www.marketwatch.com/story/people-are-spending-most-of-their-waking-hours-staring-at-screens-2018-08-01.

Goldstein, E. Bruce. "Individual Differences In Perception." *Encyclopedia of Perception*, 1st ed. Thousand Oaks, CA: Sage Publications, 2010.

Hasler, Gregor, Jan Willem van der Veen, Christian Grillon, Wayne C. Drevets, and Jun Shen. "Effect of Acute Psychological Stress on Prefrontal GABA Concentration Determined by Proton Magnetic Resonance Spectroscopy." *The American Journal of Psychiatry* 167, no. 10 (October 2010): 1226–31. https://doi.org/10.1176/appi.ajp.2010.09070994.

Hebb, D. O. *The Organization of Behavior: A Neuropsychological Theory* (New York: Wiley, 1949).

Hornig, Christopher D., and Richard J. McNally. "Panic Disorder and Suicide Attempt: A Reanalysis of Data from the Epidemiologic Catchment Area Study." *The British Journal of Psychiatry* 167, no. 1 (July 1995): 76–79. https://doi.org/10.1192/bjp.167.1.76.

Howe, David. "Parent-Reported Problems in 211 Adopted Children: Some Risk and Protective Factors." *Journal of Child Psychology and Psychiatry and Allied Disciplines* 38, no. 4 (1997): 401–11. https://doi.org/10.1111/j.1469-7610.1997.tb01525.x.

Kessler, Ronald C., Patricia Berglund, Olga Demler, Robert Jin, Kathleen R. Merikangas, and Ellen E. Walters. "Lifetime Prevalence and Age-of-Onset Distributions of DSM-IV Disorders in the National Comorbidity Survey Replication." *Archives of General Psychiatry* 62, no. 6 (July 2005): 593–602. https://doi.org/10.1001/archpsyc.62.6.593.

Kiecolt-Glaser, Janice K., Martha A. Belury, Rebecca Andridge, William B. Malarkey, and Ronald Glaser. "Omega-3 Supplementation Lowers Inflammation and Anxiety in Medical Students: A Randomized Controlled Trial." *Brain, Behavior and Immunity* 25, no. 8 (November 2011): 1725–34. https://doi.org/10.1016/j.bbi.2011.07.229.

Koenig, Harold, Harvey Jay Cohen, and Linda K. George. "Attendance at Religious Services, Interleukin-6, and Other Biological Parameters of Immune Function in Older Adults." *The International Journal of Psychiatry in Medicine* 27, no. 3 (January 1997): 233–50. https://doi.org/10.2190/40NF-Q9Y2-0GG7-4WH6.

Konrath, Sara H., William J. Chopik, Courtney K. Hsing, and Ed O'Brien. "Changes in Adult Attachment Styles in American College Students Over Time: A Meta-Analysis." *Personality and Social Psychology Review* 18, no. 4 (2014): 326–48. https://doi.org/10.1177/10 88868314530516.

Kushner, M. G., R. Krueger, B. Frye, and J. Peterson. "Epidemiological Perspectives on Co-Occurring Anxiety Disorder and Substance Use Disorder." *Anxiety and Substance Use Disorders: The Vicious Cycle of Comorbidity.* Edited by S. H. Stewart and P. J. Conrod. New York: Springer, 2008.

Le Roux, Hillary, Margaret Gatz, and Julie Loebach Wetherell. "Age at Onset of Generalized Anxiety Disorder in Older Adults." *The American Journal of Geriatric Psychiatry* 13, no. 1 (January 2005): 23–30. https://doi.org/10.1176/appi.ajgp.13.1.23.

Levine, Amir, and Rachel Heller. *Attached: The New Science of Adult Attachment and How It Can Help You Find—and Keep—Love.* New York: Penguin Random House, 2010.

Lieberman, Matthew D., Naomi I. Eisenberger, Molly J. Crockett, Sabrina M. Tom, Jennifer H. Pfeifer, and Baldwin M. Way. "Putting Feelings into Words." *Psychological Science* 18, no. 5 (May 2007): 421–28. https://doi.org/10.1111/j.1467-9280.2007.01916.x.

Liebrenz, Michael, Marie-Therese Gehring, Anna Buadze, and Carol Caflisch. "High-Dose Benzodiazepine Dependence: A Qualitative Study of Patients' Perception on Cessation and Withdrawal." *Boston Medical Center Psychiatry* 15, no. 116 (May 2015). https://doi .org/10.1186/s12888-015-0493-y.

Linehan, Marsha M. *DBT Skills Training Manual*, 2nd ed. New York: Guilford Press, 2015.

Mayo Clinic Staff. "Anxiety Disorders." Mayo Clinic. Last modified May 4, 2018. https://www.mayoclinic.org/diseases-conditions/anxiety /symptoms-causes/syc-20350961.

Meyers, David G., and Nathan C. DeWall. *Exploring Psychology*, 10th ed. New York: Worth, 2016.

Miller, G. E. "The U.S. Is the Most Overworked Developed Nation in the World." *20 Something Finance.* Last modified January 2, 2018. https://20somethingfinance.com/american-hours-worked-productiv ity-vacation.

Morris, William. *The American Heritage Dictionary of the English Language*, new college ed. Boston: Houghton Mifflin, 1981.

Murphy, Michelle, and Julian G. Mercer. "Diet-Regulated Anxiety." *International Journal of Endocrinology* (2013): 1–9. https://doi.org/10.1155/2013/701967.

Na, Hae-Ran, Eun-Ho Kang, Jae-Hon Lee, and Bum-Hee Yu. "The Genetic Basis of Panic Disorder." *Journal of Korean Medical Science* 26, no. 6 (May 2011): 701–10. https://doi.org/10.3346/jkms.2011.26.6.701.

Nerurkar, Aditi, Asaf Bitton, Roger Davis, and Russell Phillips. "When Physicians Counsel about Stress: Results of a National Study." *JAMA Internal Medicine* 173, no. 1 (November 2012): 76–77. https://doi:10.1001/2013.jamainternmed.480.

Neuvonen, Elisa, Minna Rusanen, Alina Solomon, Tiia Ngandu, Tiina Laatikainen, Hilkka Soininen, Miia Kivipelto, and Anna-Maija Tolppanen. "Late-Life Cynical Distrust, Risk of Incident Dementia, and Mortality in a Population-Based Cohort." *Neurology* 82, no. 24 (May 2014): 2205–12. https://doi.org/10.1212/WNL.0000000000000528.

Ophir, Eyal, Clifford Nass, and Anthony D. Wagner. "Cognitive Control in Media Multitaskers." *Proceedings of the National Academy of Science* 106, no. 37 (September 2009): 15583–87. https://doi.org/10.1073/pnas.0903620106.

Pargament, Kenneth, Harold G. Koenig, Nalini Tarakeshwar, and June Hahn. "Religious Coping Methods as Predictors of Psychological, Physical and Spiritual Outcomes among Medically Ill Elderly Patients: a Two-Year Longitudinal Study." *Journal of Health Psychology* 9, no. 6 (November 2004): 713–30. https://doi.org/10.1177/1359105304045366.

Prochaska, James O., and Carlo C. DiClemente. "Stages and Processes of Self-Change in Smoking: Toward an Integrative Model of Change." *Journal of Consulting and Clinical Psychology* 51, no. 5 (June 1983): 390–95.

Rachman, Stanley. "Betrayal: A Psychological Analysis." *Behavioral Research and Therapy* 48, no. 4 (April 2010): 304–11. https://doi.org/10.1016/j.brat.2009.12.002.

Ravindran, Lakshmi N., and Murray B. Stein. "The Pharmacologic Treatment of Anxiety Disorders: A Review of Progress." *The*

Journal of Clinical Psychiatry 71, no. 7 (July 2010): 839–54. https://doi.org/10.4088/JCP.10r06218blu.

Rudolph, Uwe, and Frédéric Knoflach. "Beyond Classical Benzodiazepines: Novel Therapeutic Potential of GABA[A] Receptor Subtypes." *Nature Reviews Drug Discovery* 10, no. 9 (July 2011): 685–97. https://doi.org/10.1038/nrd3502.

Samuelsson, Gillis, C. McCamish-Svensson, B. Hagberg, G. Sundström, and Ove Dehlin. "Incidence and Risk Factors for Depression and Anxiety Disorders: Results from a 34-Year Longitudinal Swedish Cohort Study." *Aging and Mental Health* 9, no. 6 (November 2005): 571–75. https://doi.org/10.1080/13607860500193591.

Sartori, Simone B., N. Whittle, A. Hetzenauer, and N. Singewald. "Magnesium Deficiency Induces Anxiety and HPA Axis Dysregulation: Modulation by Therapeutic Drug Treatment." *Neuropharmacology* 62, no. 1 (January 2012): 304–12. https://doi.org/10.1016/j.neuropharm.2011.07.027.

Schacter, Daniel L. *Searching for Memory: The Brain, the Mind, and the Past.* New York: Basic Books, 1996.

Schommer, Marlene. "Effects of Beliefs about the Nature of Knowledge on Comprehension." *Journal of Educational Psychology* 82, no. 3 (September 1990): 498–504. https://doi.org/10.1037/0022-0663.82.3.498.

Shür, Remmelt R., Luc W. R. Draisma, Jannie P. Wijnen, Marco P. Boks, Martijn G. J. C. Koevoets, Marian Joëls, Dennis W. Klomp, René S. Kahn, and Christiaan H. Vinkers. "Brain GABA Levels across Psychiatric Disorders: A Systematic Literature Review and Meta-Analysis of (1) H-MRS Studies." *Human Brain Mapping* 37, no. 9 (September 2016): 337–52. https://doi.org/10.1002/hbm.23244.

Smith, Joshua P., and Sarah W. Book. "Anxiety and Substance Use Disorders: A Review." *The Psychiatric Times* 25, no. 10 (October 2008): 19.

Spear, Linda. "The Adolescent Brain and Age-Related Behavioral Manifestations." *Neuroscience Biobehavioral Review* 24, no. 4 (June 2000): 417–63.

Strawbridge, W. J. "Frequent Attendance at Religious Services and Mortality Over 28 Years." *American Journal of Public Health* 87, no. 6 (June 1997): 957–61.

Stuart, Scott, and Michael Robertson. *Interpersonal Psychotherapy: A Clinician's Guide*. Boca Raton, FL: Taylor and Francis Group, 2012.

The American Institute of Stress. "What is Stress?" https://www.stress.org/what-is-stress.

The Princeton Language Institute, ed. "Patient." *Roget's 21st Century Thesaurus*, 3rd ed. New York: Philip Lief Group, 2013. Accessed February 2019. https://www.thesaurus.com/browse/patient?s=t.

Tindle, Hilary, Yue-Fang Chang, Lewis H. Kuller, JoAnn E. Manson, Jennifer G. Robinson, Milagros C. Rosal, Greg J. Siegle, and Karen A. Matthews. "Optimism, Cynical Hostility, and Incident Coronary Heart Disease and Mortality in the Women's Health Initiative." *Circulation* 120, no. 8 (September 2009): 656–62. https:doi.org/10.1161/circulationaha.108.827642.

Torabi, Mozhgan, Mahnaz Kesmati, Hooman Eshagh Harooni, and Hosein Najafzadeh Varzi. "Effects of Nano and Conventional Zinc Oxide on Anxiety-Like Behavior in Male Rats." *Indian Journal of Pharmacology* 45, no. 5 (September 2013): 508–12. https://doi.org/10.4103/0253-7613.117784.

Wikipedia. s.v. "betrayal." Last modified February 19, 2019. https://en.wikipedia.org/wiki/Betrayal.

William, Morris. *The American Heritage Dictionary of the English Language*. Boston: Houghton Mifflin, 1981.

Wilson, Timothy D. *Strangers to Ourselves: Discovering the Adaptive Unconscious*. Boston: Harvard University Press, 2004.

Jean Holthaus, LISW, LMSW, has practiced as a clinical social worker since 1995 and also manages two outpatient clinics at Pine Rest Christian Mental Health Services. She earned a BA in elementary education from the University of Northern Iowa and was an elementary and junior high teacher for ten years prior to getting her master of social work degree from the University of Iowa. She is passionate about equipping individuals, families, and churches and frequently speaks and presents workshops on a variety of mental health topics. She has two adult children.

Discover MORE content from
Jean!

ManagingWorryAndAnxiety.com